MONIKA WIESAK

Michael Jackson: The Man, the Music, the Controversy

First edition

ISBN: 979-8-9865568-3-3

This book was professionally typeset on Reedsy.
Find out more at reedsy.com

To Collie
Thank you for your eternal encouragement and support

Contents

Preface

Art is political in the most profound sense. - John F. Kennedy

It was January 31, 1993. I was a young pre-teen enjoying the first half of the Super Bowl, excitedly awaiting the halftime show. Michael Jackson was set to perform, and I could not wait to see his chosen song set. He was different from the other artists. Even as a child, I could sense the depth and message in his music. The first song of his I had ever heard was "Man in the Mirror," and though I could not make out all the lyrics, I could feel the sincerity in his voice. He urged me to be kinder, gentler, and more empathetic to those forgotten by society.

When halftime arrived, he shot up onto the stage from underneath and stood utterly silent—frozen like a statue for a full ninety seconds—while the crowd cheered wildly. Not many artists, then or now, can command a stage simply by standing still in silence. When the music finally began, he performed two sets. The first was a medley culminating with the hit song "Black or White," the lyrics urging Americans to end their obsession with race. Then came the main set. He brought on stage children dressed in the native wear of their home countries—spanning all the continents—and sang "Heal the World." In introducing the song, he said, "Today, we stand together all around the world, joined in a common purpose to remake the planet into a haven of joy and understanding and goodness. No one should have to suffer, especially our children." When given a public platform—arguably the biggest—Michael Jackson chose to use it as a unifying force. It was a touching moment, a glimpse of what could be possible.

President John F. Kennedy once said about the power of art:

> Art knows no national boundaries. Genius can speak in any tongue, and the entire world will hear it and listen. ... The musician continues the quiet work of centuries, building bridges of experience between peoples, reminding man of the universality of his feelings and desires and despairs, and reminding him that the forces that unite are deeper than those that divide. Thus, art ... is political in the most profound sense—not as a weapon in the struggle, but as an instrument of understanding of the futility of struggle between those who share man's fate.[1]

Michael Jackson himself stated a week after the Super Bowl, "I believe that all art has as its ultimate goal the union between the material and the spiritual, the human and the divine. I believe that to be the reason for the very existence of art."[2]

Then the unthinkable happened. A mere half year later, the press broke a story that forever changed Michael Jackson's life, his career trajectory, and the influence he and his music could exert over society. By 1993, the press had been harsh towards Michael for some time, but nothing could match what was about to happen. He was accused of molesting a child. It seemed unreal. It sounded like one of the many false stories spread about Jackson—but the press was taking it seriously. Indeed, not only were they taking it seriously, but many were reporting on it as if it were a foregone conclusion. Thus began the downfall of one of the biggest icons in world history.

The mainstream narrative written about this fall from grace leads to the inevitable conclusion that it was Jackson's fault—that he was a sick and depraved man whose own actions led to his downfall. But is that really what happened? Was there ever any concrete evidence that Jackson molested children? Do the allegations made about him over the years hold up under scrutiny? And if they do not hold up, why have many in the corporate media paraded the accusations as fact for decades? Did Michael Jackson fall from grace, or was he taken down?

The story of Michael Jackson offers illuminating insight into the world of entertainment, media, and power. It raises the question: How free are artists to express themselves? In one of Michael's most controversial songs, "They Don't Care About Us," he responded to the allegations by asking what happened to his rights. Was the promise of liberty a mere illusion?

While he may not have been given a fair platform from which to defend himself, he responded in a very powerful way through the only avenue he had—his music. Indeed, his art gives tremendous insight into his story.

Things are not always what they seem. Before passing judgment on another, we should always ensure we have all the facts first—especially when it comes to criminal allegations. Nothing should be taken as self-evident, and everything should be scrutinized. Michael Jackson often said, "Lies run sprints. The truth runs marathons." It is not easy to combat a mountain of lies, but it can and must be done. In a world of divide and conquer Michael Jackson's music has always been a threat. But it is needed more than ever—in our highly divisive times—to remind us of our shared humanity. I hope this book not only recalls for the reader (or perhaps introduces for the first time) the beauty of Michael Jackson's art and the hopefulness and purity in his message but also gives the comfort to enjoy it with the confidence that Michael was his music—kind, thoughtful, and empathetic.

1

A Star is Born

I quickly went over to him because I wanted to see his birth certificate. I did not believe that someone that young could have that much feeling and soul. - Singer Smokey Robinson

Michael Joseph Jackson was born on August 29, 1958, in Gary, Indiana, approximately 30 miles southeast of Chicago. He was the seventh of nine children born to Joseph and Katherine Jackson. Katherine was a devout Jehovah's Witness who worked part-time as a store clerk, and Joseph worked at a local steel mill.[3] No one could have fathomed on that day the talent this baby would come to possess. That God-given talent combined with hard work would one day turn him into arguably one of the most famous human beings to ever walk the planet.

Michael's connection to music was apparent almost from birth. His mother shared how when he was a baby, he would dance to the rhythm of the washing machine. "He would be down there dancing, sucking his bottle to the squeaking of the washer. ... He just loved music, and he loved to dance."[4]

It did not take long for Michael's singular talent to become evident. He began performing at the tender age of five.[5] When he was in the first grade, he sang publicly for the first time at a school event. The joyous response from the audience and his teachers overwhelmed him. He later reflected that at that moment, he felt confused. He did not grasp that his talent was unique. He stated:

> I just sang and danced and didn't understand why people were applauding, clapping, and screaming, you really don't, you don't know why.[6] ... When you have a special ability, you don't realize it because you think everybody else has the same gift you have. When I used to sing at such a young age, people were so inspired by my singing, and they loved it, and I didn't realize why they were clapping or crying or start[ing] to scream; I really, truly didn't.[7] ... When you get older, you start to have a more rounded personality, your brain starts to grow, you start reasoning, and understanding more things and researching.[8]

Soon after Michael's first-grade performance, his father began rehearsing him with his brothers. He entered them into talent competitions and had them practice each night after school.[9] They would sometimes drive hundreds of miles to participate in talent shows.[10] They would make trips to Chicago for amateur night. They would perform at night clubs, including strip clubs.[11] Michael reflected on one such evening:

> I saw something that really blew me away because I didn't know things like that existed. ... This one girl with gorgeous eyelashes and long hair came out and did her routine. ... All of a sudden, at the end, she took off her wig, pulled a pair of big oranges out of her bra, and revealed that she was a hard-faced guy under all that makeup. That blew me away. I was only a child and couldn't even conceive of anything like that. ... I'm just a little kid, standing in the wings, watching this crazy stuff.[12]

Being exposed to an adult world at such a young age profoundly impacted Michael for the rest of his life.

Michael and his brothers performed relentlessly for several years before they released their first recorded song, when Michael was nine years old. "Big Boy," was released by Steeltown and played on local radio stations.[13] After winning amateur night three weeks in a row at the Royal Theater in Chicago, the brothers got their first big break when, as a prize, they got to open for Gladys Knight and the Pips. Knight then talked to the group about auditioning for Motown, a major record label.[14] Before the audition, however, the group went to New York City and won amateur night at the Apollo, no small feat.[15] Then, in the summer of 1968, they drove to Detroit to audition for Motown. The head and founder of Motown, Barry Gordy, was blown away by the audition and signed the brothers to a recording contract.[16] At the audition, Gordy had Michael sing the Smokey Robinson song "Who's Loving You." He described Michael's performance as being beyond his years, stating, "He sang it with the sadness and passion of a man who had been living the blues and heartbreak his whole life."[17] Indeed, Michael was very sensitive to the pain of others from a young age. His mother recalled, "I can remember Marlon, his older brother, being sick. ... Michael was standing there holding his hand, a boy of three years old, and crying ... because his brother was sick."[18]

Smokey Robinson recounted the moment he first heard Michael's recording of his song:

> I thought to myself, now they have pulled a fast one on us because this boy cannot possibly be ten years old. This song is about somebody who has somebody who loved them, but they treated them bad. They treated them so bad until they lost them. And now they are paying the price of wanting somebody back that they treated bad and lost. How could he possibly know these things? I quickly went over to him because I wanted to see his birth certificate. I did not believe that someone that young could have that much feeling and soul.[19]

Robinson often called Michael "an old soul in a little body." Later in life, Michael recounted, "I remember hearing that all the time when I was little. They used to call me a forty-five-year-old midget. ... Some people say, when you were little, and you started to sing, did you know you were that good? I never thought about it; I just did it, and it came out."[20]

Michael and his brothers moved to Los Angeles after signing the Motown recording contract. For the first year and a half, they lived part-time with Barry Gordy and part-time with singer Diana Ross, after which their parents bought a house in California.[21] Not long after moving to California, Michael stopped going to formal school and began being tutored. When asked when he finished formal schooling, Michael replied:

> I was very young, I think it was ... probably the fourth or fifth [grade], and then I had tutoring the rest of my life because we did so many tours and concerts and TV shows and things, all the albums and recordings. We would have three hours of schooling, and then we would do the concerts, and then we would travel to another state or another country, and then we'd do some concerts again, and then it would be time to record another ... album. So, in my youth ... I was always busy.[22]

The Jackson 5 was the official group name given to Michael and his brothers. They released their first song, "I Want You Back," in November 1969. It sold two million copies in six weeks and went to number one on the charts. Their next single, "ABC," came out in March 1970, sold two million records in just three weeks, and also took the top spot on the charts. Their third single, "The Love You Save," became yet another number-one hit in June of 1970.[23] The Jackson 5 had hit the big time.

But not all was rosy. Although Michael did not become a household name until 1969, he had been performing heavily already for five years. He stated later in life, "I don't remember not performing."[24] Michael said of his youth,

"I'd go to a recording studio and record, and I'd record for hours and hours until it was time to go to sleep. ... I remember going to the recording studio; there was a park across the street, and I'd see all the children playing, and they'd be rooting and making noise, and I would cry. It would make me sad that I would have to go and work instead." He elaborated:

> There were times when I'd have great times with my brothers—pillow fights and things—but ... I used to always cry from loneliness. ... When I was little, it was always work, work, work, from one concert to the next. If it wasn't a concert, it was the recording studio. If it wasn't that, it was a TV show, or interviews, or picture sessions. It was always something to do. ... I loved show business, and I still love show business, but there are times when you want to play and have some fun, and that part did make me sad. I remember one time we were getting ready to go to South America, and everybody was packed up in the cars, ready to leave and go, and the plane was about to take off, and I hid. I was crying while I was hiding because I really did not want to go. I wanted to play. I did not want to go.[25]

Though Michael often said his dad was abusive and demanding, he developed at least somewhat of an understanding of his father later in life. He stated in a 2001 speech at Oxford University:

> Despite my earlier denials, I am forced to admit that he must have loved me. He did love me. And I know that. ... I've started reflecting on the fact that my father grew up in the South in a very poor family. He came of age during the Depression. And his own father struggled to feed his children and showed little affection towards his family and raised him ... with an iron fist. Who could imagine what it was like to grow up a poor black man in the South, robbed of dignity, bereft of hope, struggling to become a man in a world that saw my father as subordinate? ... My father moved to

5

Indiana and had a large family of his own, working long hours at the steel mills, work that kills the lungs and humbles the spirit, all to support his family. Is it any wonder that he found it difficult to expose his feelings? Is it any mystery that he hardened his heart, that he raised the emotional ramparts? And most of all, is it any wonder why he pushed his sons so hard to succeed as performers so that they could be saved from what he knew to be a life of indignity and poverty?

I have begun to see that even my father's harshness was a kind of love—an imperfect love, to be sure, but love, nonetheless. He pushed me because he loved me because he wanted no man to ever look down upon his offspring. And now, with time, rather than bitterness, I feel blessing. In the place of anger, I have found absolution. And in the place of revenge, I have found reconciliation.[26]

Michael told Geraldo Rivera in 2005:

At this season in your life, at this stage, I think you tend to appreciate who your parents are more. You almost tend to retract everything, where you are in your life. All the wonderful things they instilled in you. You start to see them come forth, to take fruition in your life. ... I'm very much like my father in a lot of ways. He's very strong. He's a warrior. He's always taught us to be courageous, to be confident, and to believe in our ideals ... and you never give up, no matter what.[27]

Michael was a phenomenally successful performer at a young age. But like everyone else, he did not stay young forever. Unlike other teens, Michael experienced his awkward years in the limelight. For someone so sensitive, it was not an easy transition for him. His appearance began to really change at age fourteen, and this public transition deeply impacted him. He explained:

People who didn't know me would come into a room expecting to be introduced to cute little Michael Jackson, and they'd walk right past me. I would say, "I'm Michael," and they would look doubtful. ... I was not the person they expected or even wanted to see. Adolescence is hard enough, but imagine having your own natural insecurities about the changes your body is undergoing heightened by the negative reaction of others.[28]

Michael's friend and personal portrait artist, David Nordahl, explained how these early years impacted Michael:

He always considered himself to be extremely ugly. One of the things that really planted that seed in his head was he had become a teenager, and of course, everybody started watching Michael when he was a little kid. He was a delightful little act. ... All of a sudden, you spurt up, you're tall, you don't look the same anymore. He had terrible acne. ... He was playing at a concert somewhere, and when he arrived, people said, "There he is, there's Michael! There's Michael!" People said, "No, that's not Michael! That's not Michael!"[29]

In the fall of 1971, Michael released his first solo album, *Got to Be There*.[30] Despite the solo release, he continued to record and perform with his brothers. However, by 1974, the brothers began to feel disenchanted with Motown. Michael informed Motown that the group wanted to write and produce their own songs, but Motown would not agree to such stipulations.[31] As a result, the group parted ways with the label and signed on to Epic Records. As part of the transition, the group was forced to change their name from the Jackson 5 to The Jacksons as the original name was Motown's registered trademark.[32] The Jacksons released their first album under Epic in 1976 and continued to release albums until the mid-1980s. The albums with his brothers did not stop Michael from releasing solo albums during the same period. He released a few more solo albums throughout the 1970s as an adolescent and released his first solo album as an adult in 1979, the Grammy-winning *Off the Wall*.

While *Off the Wall* was a hit, Michael's 1982 follow-up album, *Thriller*, catapulted him to super-stardom. The album spawned multiple hit songs and spent an unprecedented thirty-seven weeks at the top spot on the Billboard charts.[33] In some ways, this was the pinnacle of Michael's career, not in terms of his artistry—arguably, his music got better with time, and it certainly gained more depth—but it was a time when his music was mega successful, and the media was still relatively kind to him. He was the young superstar everyone loved.

2

Unexpected Challenges

The press—they wait with knives. - Michael Jackson

After the massive success of *Thriller*, Michael Jackson's life and career held immense promise. The 1980s were going to be his decade. However, it did not take long for various difficulties to present themselves. The post-*Thriller* era was not free of struggle.

In early 1984, Michael suffered a horrific accident that forever altered the trajectory of his life. While filming a stage performance for a commercial, his hair caught on fire due to magnesium flash bombs exploding near his head. He suffered second- and third-degree burns on his scalp. A doctor told him it was a miracle he was alive. A fireman informed him that he was lucky that his clothes did not catch on fire and that his face was not burnt and disfigured.[34] As a result of the accident, Michael was introduced to painkillers for the first time. The burns continued to cause him suffering throughout his life, and while most of his natural hair remained, he had to attach hair pieces to cover the approximately palm-sized burned area of his scalp. He could no longer grow hair where the burn scars were.[35] Michael's hairstylist, Carol LaMere, stated that doctors told Michael they could fix the burn area so he would not need hair pieces, but their attempts only worsened it.[36] The burns likely led to Michael's vitiligo or exacerbated a nascent case. Vitiligo is a disease

9

that causes the skin to lose its pigmentation. Common triggers of vitiligo are burns and chemical exposures.[37] Vitiligo can also be aggravated by other autoimmune diseases, such as lupus, which Michael was diagnosed with in 1983.[38] Overexposure to artificial lights can aggravate lupus.[39] Michael had been performing under harsh spotlights from a young age. Vitiligo spreads in uneven patches across the skin. Makeup is often used to even out the skin, and bleaching treatments can be prescribed if the vitiligo becomes widespread. Debbie Rowe, a medical assistant to Michael's dermatologist, Arnold Klein, spoke of how traumatic the burns, lupus, and vitiligo were for Michael: "They would be difficult for anybody, even singularly. But for him to have it—he's very shy. So, for him to have all of this going on and to be in the public was ... really, really difficult for him. ... He was worried people would see the disease or disfigurement before they would see him working."[40]

The media for decades implied that Michael was intentionally bleaching his skin. However, many people around Michael, including those who worked on his makeup and hair,[41] confirmed he had vitiligo. Friend David Nordahl said of the first time he met Michael in 1988, "Because he didn't have makeup on, I noticed the vitiligo. It was on the right-hand side of his face, and down his neck, and also on the back of his hand. I didn't know how far it went up his arm because he had a long-sleeved shirt on."[42] Musical collaborator Matt Forger stated that some people refuse to believe that Michael had vitiligo, "But that was indeed the case because I literally saw that at an earlier stage. I saw that when we were working on the *Bad* album [during the mid-1980s]. ... And he was very embarrassed by it. ... When you're in those very formative years when you're very young ... this can be tremendously traumatic." Forger mentioned that Michael would wear long sleeves to cover up the vitiligo as best he could, but he did not wear makeup while working in the recording studio.[43] He did, however, wear makeup when performing or making public appearances. Friend David Nordahl explained:

The vitiligo spread and spread and spread, and it was difficult for him when he had to appear in public or to perform to get the right kind of makeup because ... where the vitiligo was, that skin was white, not like Caucasian white, it was white like a refrigerator, snow white. So, in the beginning, he did use darker makeup to cover that, but then as that spread, it got more and more difficult to make that white skin the color of the rest of his skin, so he would have to go to lighter and lighter and lighter makeup because ... when you sweat ... you don't want these white lines running down your face.[44]

In recent years, numerous pictures of Michael have leaked on the internet where the vitiligo patches are clearly visible on his skin. Indeed, his autopsy report in 2009 confirmed that he had vitiligo. It stated he had "patches of light and dark pigmented areas" and listed vitiligo as the official diagnosis.[45] Multiple doctors who treated Michael have also testified under oath that he had vitiligo.

Nordahl reflected on how the press treated Michael's suffering from the disease:

> They treated him without any respect for the fact that he is a human being. ... Fairly early on, the press understood that Michael had vitiligo. ... They still hammered on this fact that he was trying to be white and that he was bleaching his skin to be a white person. The skin bleachings were because of the vitiligo. ... When he would go outside ... he would have long sleeves on, he would wear his hat, and he would either put a bandana or something over his face, or he would carry an umbrella or all those things because he could not let sun hit that skin. He was so susceptible to cancer because there was no protection. ... It's a very serious condition. ... And to be so cruel to someone that was afflicted that way is unforgivable. It would be different if the press didn't know about it, but they knew about it for a long time, for years and years and years. They

knew ... they absolutely knew.[46]

Michael responded to the rumors in a 1993 interview:

> I have a skin disorder; I cannot help it. When people make up stories that I don't want to be who I am, it hurts me. It is a problem for me. I can't control it. But what about all the millions of people— let's reverse it—what about all the millions of people who sit out in the sun to become darker, to become other than what they are? Nobody says nothing about that. ... We're trying to control it, and using makeup evens it out because it creates blotches on the skin. I have to even out my skin. But you know what's funny? Why is that so important? That's not important to me. I'm a great fan of art. I love Michelangelo. If I had a chance to talk to him or read about him, I would want to know about what inspired him to become who he is, the anatomy of his craftsmanship, not about who he went out with last night or why he decided to sit out in the sun so long. ... That's what's important to me.[47]

There is no doubt dealing with vitiligo was a very traumatic experience for Michael. Doctor Patrick Treacy recalled, "I remember one time him opening up one of the dermatology texts I have, it's about three hundred or four hundred pages long, and he came along a picture of a black African child with vitiligo ... and he says to me, 'Nobody can understand the pain and the mental anguish that child is going through.'"[48]

It is almost certain that the burns either led to or aggravated an existing case of vitiligo. The burns also led to various surgical attempts to repair the scars. Michael also appears to have had plastic surgery on his nose during this period. No one will ever know why he elected to have these surgeries, but some factors that perhaps played a role were: 1) insecurities due to traumatic experiences in his teenage years of being ridiculed for his looks; 2) being under a constant spotlight; 3) uncontrollable changes in appearance due to the depigmentation of his skin, his lupus, and the loss of parts of his hair and trying to adjust to those changes (according to one doctor, Michael's lupus destroyed part of the skin of his nose, and so his nasal surgeries were really reconstructive to achieve a normal appearance);[49] and 4) his perfectionism as an artist, with his appearance on stage being a part of that art. It is easy for a layperson to judge. But certainly someone who had experienced constant teasing and uncontrollable changes to his appearance—under very public scrutiny—and was constantly in the spotlight would understandably have felt tremendous pressure under such circumstances.

From July to December 1984, Michael toured with his brothers for the final time. Although he was performing with his brothers, he performed many of his solo songs during the tour. He donated his entire proceeds from the tour to charity.[50] It would not be the last time he would do so.

Soon after the end of the tour, Michael's musical producer, Quincy Jones, asked him to write a charity song to raise funds for the famine in Ethiopia. Michael got together with Lionel Richie, and the two wrote the song "We Are the World." The lyrics called for unity, generosity, and kindness. The song was recorded by a slew of top artists and released on March 7, 1985.[51] It sold over 20 million copies and raised over $60 million in relief funds.[52]

In August 1985, Michael purchased ATV Music Publishing, which held the rights to over 4,000 songs, including over 250 Beatles songs. Michael paid $47.5 million for the catalog. He later merged the catalog with Sony in 1995, who themselves owned rights to a slew of songs. This merger created the Sony/ATV Catalog, with Michael holding a 50 percent stake in what was now a much more extensive music catalog than the one he'd originally purchased. Sony paid Michael $100 million for the deal. Michael Jackson's estate ultimately sold his 50 percent stake in the catalog in 2016 for $750 million, a price many considered a bargain.[53] Michael always vowed he would never sell the catalog. As a result, many fans were disappointed when his estate sold his stake, particularly given they had already cleared almost all of Michael's debts prior to the sale. The catalog allowed Michael to make money off other artists' music, generating a constant income stream in addition to the income from his own music.

Up until 1985, Michael had received relatively fair press coverage. However, in 1985, the press began printing negative stories about him in earnest.[54] The British tabloid *The Sun* coined the derogatory moniker "Wacko Jacko." Other media outlets followed suit.[55] The term "Jacco" was East London slang for "monkey," and one has to ask if the use of this language was intentional.

The negative and demeaning stories only increased in volume and intensity as the years passed. Eventually, the negative coverage bled from the tabloid press into the mainstream press. Initially, the stories were silly. With time, they became cruel. It is difficult to deduce the source of this merciless press treatment, but there is no doubt that throughout the latter half of his life, Michael was treated by the media more harshly than arguably any other public figure. Was it his mega success and popularity that triggered the initial negative stories? Was it his crossover from a mere musician who worked for others to the owner of lucrative and highly sought-after music publishing? Was it his changing appearance, largely triggered by the burns, lupus, and vitiligo? Was it the rising conscientiousness in his music? *Thriller* was a fun album, but with "We Are the World" and other songs that would follow in a similar vein, Michael's music was beginning to acquire meaning. Was it his unique persona differing him so significantly from other celebrities that triggered the initial press attacks? Or was it purely profit-driven? It was likely a combination of all these factors.

Michael himself stated of the rising negative press coverage:

> You had [black artists like] Belafonte. You had Sammy. You had Nat "King" Cole. People loved their music, but they didn't get adulation; they didn't get the crying. I was the first one to break the ice, break the mold, where white girls, Scottish girls, Irish girls

[were] screaming, "I'm in love with you" ... and a lot of the white press, they didn't like that. And that's why they started the stories, "He's weird, he's gay, he sleeps in a hyperbaric chamber, he wants to buy the elephant man bones"—anything that turned people against me. They tried their hardest. I've been an ambassador of goodwill all over the world. ... We do "Heal the World." ... What I don't understand is just singing about sex and, "I want to get in a hot tub with you baby and rub you all over" ... but I get battered in the press as the weirdo. ... And the press—they wait with knives. They try to shred me apart. Because when you're the top-selling artist of all time ... you're the target. ... Get him down. Get him.[56]

The more popular I became, the more rumors that were created, none of which were true. ... They called me weird overnight, strange, wacko. ... None of that stuff is true.[57]

Michael also spoke of how intrusive the press could be:

If you go to a bookstore ... every book you buy they want to know: Why are you buying this? ... Why is he reading this? ... So you can't go anywhere. ... So, they're so quick to call you strange and weird, but it's almost as if you're forced to be different because it's not a normal life.[58]

It was more than just the media that made it challenging for Michael to live a normal life. His instant recognizability whenever he ventured out in public was also exacting, though he never complained. He understood it was the "Price of Fame," as he titled one of his songs. He talked about how difficult and nearly impossible it was for him to do everyday things. He could only dream of experiencing the typical excursions that most take for granted. He excitedly spoke—in the same manner that most would talk of going to Disneyland—of what it would be like to walk through a grocery store: "I want to go to the market, one of those markets, and take one of those carts and throw some food in it and go down the aisle. I would love to do that."[59]

But normal everyday outings were not very practical for him. Not only was he recognized and immediately surrounded by large numbers of people, but they would also change as soon as they saw him. He explained, "When they see it's Michael Jackson, they change. I don't see the real thing. I want to see the real world, what it's really like."[60]

He elaborated:

> I would like to be able to go out in public and just be normal … just to get a little bit of a feeling to what it's like … to see how things are done … learn what people speak about when they're just casually talking. As soon as they see it's Michael Jackson, the conversation changes. It all becomes about me and not about the situation, the moment that's happening at that moment. I would learn a lot from that. I don't get to see that unless I disguise myself and put on a lot of things, and then they stare at me, and then … it's not the same even then.[61]

When asked if he ever wanted to lash out at the press, Michael responded, "Yeah, a lot of times, but why bring more attention to it?" When asked directly about the Wacko Jacko moniker, he replied, "I have a heart, and I have feelings. I feel that when you do that to me. It's not nice."[62] When asked if human beings too often treat each other like animals, Michael replied, "I think so. Man's inhumanity to man, I mean, that's what war is all about."[63]

Michael wrote in a note in 1987, "If a man could say nothing against a character but what he could prove, history could not be written. Animals strike not from malice but because they want to live. It is the same with those who criticize. They desire our blood, not our pain. … But have mercy, for I've been bleeding a long time now."[64] Even in these early years, Michael was already deeply affected by the brutality of the press.

3

Michael, the Man

I try to be kind and generous to people and to do what I think God wants me to do.
- Michael Jackson

Michael Jackson is probably one of the most misunderstood public figures in history. The media over the years have created an almost cartoonish image of him that barely resembles the man he was. The best way to understand a person is through those who knew him best—those who spent regular time with him. The individuals who spent extensive time with Michael all give an incredibly consistent portrayal of the man.

Many of these individuals are not known to the public. While Michael Jackson certainly had some celebrity friends, he mostly avoided the celebrity scene. Michael explained why he did not hang out much with other celebrities: "They love the limelight, and I don't have anything in common with them. They want to go clubbing. Afterward, they want to sit around and drink hard liquor and do marijuana and do all kinds of crazy things that I wouldn't do."[65]

Michael also spoke of Madonna, who was one of the most popular female performers during the 1980s:

[Madonna] was into these books. All over, a whole collection, like a library of books of women who were tied to walls. She said, "I love spanky books." Why would I want to see that, right? I think she likes shock value. ... She said, "We are going to the restaurant, and afterward, we are going to a strip bar." I said, "I am not going to a strip bar where they cross-dress." Guys who are girls. I said, "I am not going to go there." I think afterward, she wrote some mean things about me in the press.[66]

Engineer Rob Disner spoke about Madonna visiting Michael at the studio once. He recalled the encounter: "They spent a little while in his private room in the back, and then she left. When I asked Michael later about her visit, he said that she scared him. I think we all speculated that she tried to make a move on him, but Michael never said. In any event, we never saw her again after that."[67] It should be noted that Madonna, in recent years, has spoken well of Michael.

How did those around Michael view him? Did they view him as the weirdo the press portrayed him as? Quite the contrary. Those who knew him and worked with him spoke highly of him. The press gave coverage to individuals who hardly knew Michael and who were willing to spread negative gossip about him. But those who knew him well paint a very different picture. The mainstream press rarely gave interview time to those who portrayed Michael in a positive light, but podcasts in recent years have interviewed many who knew him. These interviews shed light on the man in ways that decades of press coverage failed to do.

Painter David Nordahl recounted the time he first met Michael. Michael had called him and asked if he would give him some painting lessons. The two ultimately developed a close friendship. Nordahl recalled:

We had a great conversation the first time he called me; we talked for a long time, and I felt very comfortable talking to him. ... The

18

only thing I really knew about Michael was what I'd read in the press. ... In part of my mind, even though I'd talked to him ... I still had this thought about him kind of being this frail freak. That's everything you hear, that he's weird and all this stuff, so I didn't really know what to expect when he walked through the door.[68]

Nordahl recounted how before Michael came down to see him, Michael's assistant informed him that Michael "was so excited he couldn't even sleep last night."[69] Nordahl warmly remembered:

The amazing thing is he always treated me like I was the celebrity. He was like really humble around me. He was always that way. I could never figure it out. He was just so genuine, so warm, so caring. All the time I knew Michael, all those twenty years, I never ever heard him raise his voice at anybody; never happened. He was just such a good person, just a truly deep-down good person. ... It just makes my heart ache how he was treated. What an absolutely wonderful man, and so many people know nothing about that. ... You'd hear about how weird and Wacko Jacko and all that kind of crap, and I've never met anybody who was more well-adjusted or more normal. He was just such a normal guy, so intellectual and so bright. He knew about medicine and politics and social things, just everything. ... He hardly ever watched TV, but he got all this information through books. Every time we went someplace, he would drag out boxes of books from bookstores and ship them home, and then he was anxious to go look at them. We used to sit around and look at books and stuff together. That was one of the things we did.[70]

Nordahl explained that he often forgot who he was with, but every now and then, Michael would make a swift move with his feet, like lightning, and it would hit Nordahl that he was with Michael Jackson.[71] He explained, "I was around him so much that I got used to being around him, so we'd just hang out like a couple of guys, but then he'd do something, maybe a little three-step dance or just something that yanked me back to reality, and all of a sudden I'd think, 'Jesus, I'm sitting here with Michael Jackson.'"[72]

Brad Sundberg, a studio engineer who worked with Michael for eighteen years, also expressed that Michael was "amazingly curious."[73] Michael's nephew, TJ Jackson, said of his uncle, "He loved to have fun, and he loved to understand things and ask questions."[74] Allan Scanlan, the director of maintenance at Michael's property Neverland Ranch and better known as "Big Al," corroborated these claims when he recounted one day at Neverland when Michael was asking him about the equipment used to operate the amusement park rides:

> He was listening to me like he thought there was going to be a test later. He was really intent on listening to what I was telling him. ... I guarantee you if he was alive today and we went in that room, he could tell you everything I told him. He just was really fascinated by it, and it wasn't like it had nothing to do with music or dancing ... he was just one of those people who had a thirst for knowledge in whatever you were telling him; he was interested in it.[75]

When Michael was asked during an interview what interested him most about life, he replied, "Learning, finding out about new things, exploring different worlds."[76] Sundberg discussed what Michael was like to work with as a person:

> He was so much fun to be around. I'm an American guy. It's not common that I go to work, for example, and I hug my co-workers. I mean, that's just not what dudes do. With Michael, every time I saw him, I got a hug. I got a hug hello, and I got a hug goodbye. And that softens you a little bit. If you were going to work with Michael, then you just had to let go of some of that nonsense of

pride and ego and all that. ... I genuinely loved him. ... He taught me patience, gratitude. For all of his worth and his importance, he was one of the most grateful, thankful guys I'd ever met. And I mean that right down to if somebody would loan him a pen. He'd borrowed a pen from one of the runners at the studios, and he wrote the runner a little thank-you note. I mean, that's crazy. I don't mean that to be insulting, but that's how he was. You just don't meet people like that ever. ... He was a dreamer ... he really wanted and believed that the world could be a peaceful and loving place. ... He hated sickness and poverty. ... He was so shy in the studios. ... Once he knew us, then he was fine, but if we had a stranger or somebody new in there, he was so painfully shy.[77]

Many have claimed that Michael was a prankster. Violet Gaitan, who ran security at Neverland, described one such prank: "One time he came into the office, and he showed me a lighter, and he said, 'I can't get this lighter to work,' and it looked like a normal lighter." So, she asked him, "Well, what are you trying to light?" She knew he did not smoke. She recalled, "I don't think he liked the question, and he was like, 'Just try it.'" But she kept asking him, "Why are you using this lighter if it's not working? Let's just get something that works." But Michael insisted that she try to get his lighter to work. Gaitan said, "So I tried the lighter, and of course, it shocked me, and he could not stop laughing, and I couldn't stop laughing. ... Things like that he would do that weren't harmful; they weren't going to embarrass you or anything like that. But he certainly did have fun with that kind of thing."[78]

Photographer Harrison Funk, Michael's personal photographer from the early 1980s until the mid-2000s, stated that Michael was a "very kind, loving person" and that he admired Michael "beyond belief for how he treated people." He discussed how Michael felt about the term Wacko Jacko:

At first, I think he was really taken aback by the Wacko Jacko crap. ... He hated that. ... He could not stand the Wacko Jacko stuff.

... It was very upsetting to him. ... There were moments when he laughed at it. But he was doing that for self-preservation. I don't think there was a moment when Michael really thought it was funny. ... Every single day Wacko Jacko this, Wacko Jacko that. ... People would comment to me about it. I had one person call me and say, "How is the tour with Wacko Jacko?" and I said, "Who?" I cringed ... although I was thinking these people are the wacko ones.[79]

Brad Buxer, a close musical collaborator of Michael's and the musical director of two of his tours, shared what it was like working with Michael on his music:

Michael was amazing to work with; he would never yell or get mad at you. ... He was a gentle, sweet man, and when he didn't like what somebody was doing, he would have somebody else deal with that; he would never rant or yell or anything like that. ... It was a very smooth and harmonious working environment with him; it was absolutely wonderful.[80]

Keyboardist Rory Kaplan recounted a story when he became so distracted by an incredible dance move of Michael's that he messed up what he was supposed to play on his keyboard. Michael asked him after the concert, "What happened?" Kaplan told him the truth—that he'd become engrossed in what Michael was doing—and Michael just laughed.[81]

Kevin Dorsey, who worked with Michael for twenty-five years as his vocal director, assistant musical director, and background vocalist, reflected, "Mike was the most misunderstood person that I have known in my life. ... I've never known a more generous, gentle, loving person. ... He was someone that really, really just genuinely cared about people, even if he didn't know you. ... [He was] a very giving person, a very humble person."[82] Friend Miko Brando shared that Michael was always concerned about everyone other than himself.[83] Engineer Rob Disner said that Michael "was really concerned about doing anything that would inadvertently upset anybody around him."[84]

Steven Paul Whitsitt, a photographer who worked for Michael in the 1990s, described him as "idealistic," "deeply intelligent," and "profoundly empathetic."[85] Studio engineer Rob Hoffman said Michael had "a heart of gold."[86] Choreographer Vincent Patterson described Michael as kind, patient, loving, understanding, and generous.[87] Photographer Dick Zimmerman described him as very sensitive and caring.[88] Studio engineer Brad Sundberg shared Michael's reaction to the breakout of the first Iraq War in 1990: "You could just see that it just broke his heart."[89] Bodyguard Jimmy Van Norman described Michael as "kind, loving, caring."[90] Numerous others gave similar descriptions.

Eddie Garcia, a dancer who worked with Michael on multiple music videos and concert tours, described Michael as "so sweet, … so nice to me, he always started out, 'How are you? How's your family? How's everybody doing? Is everybody good? What's going on in your life?' He was asking me stuff about myself. … It told me a lot about him as a person because he didn't have to do that." Garcia recounted his first experience of dancing on stage with Michael when Garcia was only seventeen:

> We were in Tokyo. … We were underneath the stage, and I was shaking, and he turned to me, and he goes, "Are you nervous?" And I was like, "Yeah, yeah." … And he's like, "It's good, it's good you're nervous because you care. That's important. Take this moment in." … That one conversation changed my life, that understanding how to put me at ease being inexperienced in this and not faulting me for it and then wanting to move me forward and basically building me up before I walked out on stage with one of the most famous people in the world. For him to take that moment to realize that I needed that I thought was cool.[91]

Michael's hairstylist, Carol LaMere, stated, "Anybody who's worked with him will tell you he's probably one of the nicest people … you could ever work for. … He was just so genuine. … I don't think I've met a nicer person than him. There was nothing he wouldn't do for me if I needed something. … I love him to no end."[92]

When Michael was asked how he viewed himself, he replied, "I try to be kind and generous to people and to do what I think God wants me to do. Sometimes I pray and say, 'Where do you want me to go next, God? What do I do?' So, I'm very spiritual in that way; I always have been."[93]

As has been seen, those who knew Michael and spent extensive time with him consistently portrayed him as gentle and kind—hardly the weirdo portrayed in the press. They also described him as highly intelligent. Indeed, Michael wrote and composed much of his music. He was more than just a fabulous singer who had been given catchy songs by a resourceful record company. He was a true artist, and his persona came through in his art.

4

A Better World

If you want to make the world a better place, take a look at yourself and make a change. Start with the man in the mirror. Start with yourself. Don't be looking at all the other things. Start with you. - Michael Jackson

Michael Jackson followed up the *Thriller* album with the *Bad* album, released on August 31, 1987. Despite *Spin* magazine commenting in the lead-up to the album release that Michael had gone from being "one of the most admired celebrities to one of the most absurd," the album was a smash hit. It spawned a record-breaking five number-one songs.[94] Michael kicked off the *Bad* tour on September 12, 1987. The tour continued, with breaks, until January 27, 1989. Even though he had been touring his whole life, it was Michael's first solo tour. In 2019, award-winning investigative journalist Charles Thomson recounted a story that was shared with him about the press coverage during that tour:

> I was talking about Michael Jackson on the radio, and as I left, one of the people that worked at the studio stopped me and said, "That was so interesting to hear you putting the other side to all this Michael Jackson stuff." They said, "I've got to tell you this story: I used to work at the *Today* newspaper, which was owned by Rupert Murdoch in the late 1980s, and I was in charge of their archiving. ...

My job was to collect the pages and feed the … stories into a digital archive. … And there was a story on the front page; it was 1988, and Michael Jackson was performing in the UK. And the story said that all of these fans had been really seriously injured in a terrible crush at one of his concerts. And it was just this tiny box on the front page, and I couldn't find the story inside the paper. I thought, well, something has gone wrong here. So, I spent about three hours trying to find the person that wrote the story." They eventually found the person that wrote the story, and they said to them, "Look, I'm trying to archive this story, and all there is is a headline on the front page with about three sentences, and then the rest of the story isn't in the paper. I can't understand what is going on." And the reporter said, "Yeah, that's because it didn't happen." She said, "What are you talking about?" And he said, "We have a brief from the top to rubbish Michael Jackson at every available opportunity, and if there's nothing that's actually happened that we can rubbish him with, we have to make it up." And she said she … just could not believe what the guy was saying, and he didn't seem to be very impressed about it either. He was acting like he thought this was terrible and they shouldn't be doing it. But it was interesting to hear from somebody who was in the media at that time saying they worked for a massive national newspaper, and they were instructed to smear Michael Jackson at every opportunity.[95]

This story implies that the brutal press coverage Michael received over the years was very top-down. It was not the reporters driving it. It was those in positions of power. A small number of entities control the mainstream media. Those entities likely have no interest in sharing their influence over public opinion. As such, the press was in competition with Michael. When he spoke, people across the globe listened. Indeed, anyone who is massively famous, admired, and an independent thinker is liable to be knocked down a notch or two to ensure the media's continued monopoly over public thought. On the other hand, those who consistently and unquestioningly push the narratives of the powerful are likely to be propped up by the press.

The *Bad* album was, in many ways, a fun album, just like the *Thriller* album that preceded it, but it started to display more depth. It began a trend that would grow and blossom in later albums.

In the song "Another Part of Me," Michael conveyed that humanity is one and we are all parts of the same whole. In one of his most iconic songs, "Man in the Mirror," Michael encouraged people to start with themselves if they wanted to see a better world. He declared:

> It's the same thing [John] Kennedy was talking about when he said, 'Ask not what your country can do for you; ask what you can do for your country.' … If you want to make the world a better place, take a look at yourself and make a change. Start with the man in the mirror. Start with yourself. Don't be looking at all the other things. Start with you. That's the truth. … That's what I believe.[96]

Michael expressed in an interview, "People don't look at themselves honestly. They don't look at themselves and point the finger at themselves. It's always the other guy's fault."[97] For the "Man in the Mirror" music video, Michael displayed images of those suffering as well as the images of various historical figures whom he admired, including those assassinated in preceding decades: John F. Kennedy, Robert F. Kennedy, Martin Luther King, and John Lennon. He also displayed images of their assassinations or funerals. Michael himself only appeared for a few brief seconds amongst a large crowd at the end of the video. It was unheard-of for an artist to make a music video and not appear in it. But Michael wanted the message to stand for itself.

Michael also, for the first time, began responding to his critics via his music. In the video for the song "Leave Me Alone," Michael displayed images of all the negative press stories about him as he sang, "Just leave me alone." In the lyrics to the song "Bad," he implied that the press was attacking him to cover their own atrocities. With their self-righteous criticism of others, the media can maintain moral high ground while distracting the public from the many crimes being committed worldwide. Michael then proclaimed that we have the power to transform the world into a better place, and those who disapprove of his messages were welcome to "slap" him in the face.

Indeed, Michael got figuratively slapped around for the rest of his life. Did it have anything to do with what he was saying in his music? Without question, Michael's influence was global and massive. And there is no doubt about music's effect on culture. It can be either a unifying or a divisive force. It can encourage kindness and compassion or promote anger and violence. It can encourage depth or promote superficiality. It can foster awareness or serve as a mere distraction.

5

Neverland

Once you're into the gates, you are in a very wonderful, quiet, loving place. -
Michael Jackson

Michael Jackson underwent several significant personal changes during the
Bad era. In 1987, he officially left the Jehovah's Witnesses.[98] In that same year,
he purchased Sycamore Valley Ranch, which he renamed Neverland Valley
Ranch.[99] Neverland was a 2700-acre estate of mostly wilderness situated
next to the Los Padres National Forest and near the small town of Los Olivos
in Santa Barbara County. It was an approximately two-and-a-half-hour drive
north of Los Angeles. Friend David Nordahl shared, "[Michael] absolutely
loved the ranch. ... We could drive around, we could drive golf carts, we
could walk in the woods ... and not worry about fans trying to run him
down. ... He could just be him."[100]

There are many misperceptions about Neverland. The media has portrayed it
as an extravagant expenditure. The property does include a small amusement
park, a zoo, a train station, railroad tracks, a fifty-seat movie theater, and
a video arcade, all added after Michael purchased the ranch. However,
the main house on the property was relatively modest, and Michael never
replaced it or built a new one. It was a large, but not massive, two-story,
six-bedroom house with a rustic, cabin-like feel. There were also three guest

cottages on the property. The ranch was located essentially in the wilderness.

Sound engineer Brad Sundberg, a frequent visitor to Neverland, stated that upon entering the property:

> You would never think it was the driveway of a global celebrity. There were no lawns or flowers on the drive to the main ornate gate, as we called it, and the hills were usually dry and dusty with bushy shrubs and lizards. ... Neverland wasn't really set up for a lot of traffic, as the primary roads are barely wide enough for two cars to pass each other without driving on the grass.[101]

Allan "Big Al" Scanlan worked as the maintenance director of the ranch for fifteen years, from 1990 to 2005. The ranch essentially closed in late 2005 after Michael's child molestation trial. Big Al revealed that first-time visitors to the ranch often thought they were lost when driving up to the property. He explained:

> The last few miles, you don't see anything; you're heading towards the top of this big giant mountain. So, it's out in the country, that's for sure. Then when you come in ... there's nothing big or fancy about the front gates, it doesn't say Neverland, it doesn't say anything about Michael, it's just a couple of gates and a security check.[102]

Once inside the gates, Big Al described much of the ranch as the "Wild West." He explained, "The area around the house ... is manicured like a golf course. It's gorgeous, but the whole rest of the ranch is pretty much just like it's been for hundreds and hundreds of years. It's lots of sycamore oak trees and rolling hills, and there's four hundred or five hundred head of cattle there."[103] It was not uncommon to run into wild animals on the property. Violet Gaitan worked at the ranch from 1991 to 2005, starting as a security officer and eventually rising to oversee all of Safety and Human Resources.

She told stories of all the animals the staff would encounter:

> They had swans in [the lake]. ... The swans are interesting because
> they look so beautiful out on the water and graceful. They would
> hide in the bushes and then come out after you unsuspectingly. All
> of the sudden, you'd have this swan coming out with its wingspan
> wide open, which is kind of scary; there were so many things
> there to be on your toes about ... like the swans, the wild animals
> that were there that would come out at night. ... It was scary to
> meet a skunk or a raccoon. ... I knew what to do if I came across
> someone—but animals, I didn't know what to do.

The security team did not carry any firearms at Michael's request. Gaitan,
however, was not overly concerned about trespassers accessing the main
area of the property. She explained:

> My sort of philosophy on that was ... it's very easy to get over the
> fencing, there's nothing to it, but then it takes about another half
> mile to get to the main part of the property ... let them walk that
> half mile of hill and meet up with cows and whatever else is out
> there and by the time they get to the main part of the property we'll
> be waiting, and they'll just be so tired that ... they'll be so happy
> that we picked them up.

The property was full of not only cattle but also rattlesnakes, wild boar,
mountain lions, bears, skunks, raccoons, and much more. Gaitan recounted
how it was not uncommon to run into a herd of twenty to twenty-five wild
pigs.

One night, Gaitan and another security staffer decided to experiment and
see how difficult it would be for a trespasser at night to reach the main house.
She recounted the experience, "I was scared out of my mind the whole time.
... It's terrifying." On a moonless night, the property is pitch black—so dark

one cannot even see their feet on the ground.

Michael, though, loved all the wildlife on the property. He made sure the staff understood that the land belonged as much to the animals roaming it as it did to him. He personally moved tarantulas off the road so vehicles would not run them over. Animals would sometimes wander onto the main area of the property. "We had a bear that was terrorizing the property for a while, and I don't mean he was hurting anyone; he was getting all the trash cans and dumping them over," Gaitan recalled. One night, when this bear was out, Gaitan ran into Michael and said to him, "Don't go back to the zoo; there's a bear out there right now." "I didn't finish my sentence," she said, "and he took off, and where did he go? He went right to where the bear was." She thought to herself, he is on his own; she can protect him from people, but not bears.[104]

Big Al had his own scary experience with what he thought was a bear. One of his responsibilities was to operate the steam train. He revealed that running the steam train at night was one of his favorite activities at Neverland because it felt like going back two hundred years in time.[105] He said:

> At nighttime, as soon as you pull away from the depot there by the house, the tracks cut into the side of the mountain, and you have these big giant sycamore oak trees that are a couple of hundred years old on both sides of you, and you don't see anything but the light generated from the headlight on the train and the steam blowing out from the front of it, and it was like … going back in time to the old Wild West.

He shared a story of one night when Michael was sitting at the back of the train with some guests:

> I take off, and I'm sitting there, and I'm watching the gauges, and I'm watching the water; it was nighttime. … I got to remind you

that we were out in the boonies; it's not that uncommon to see wildlife out there. There are deer and who knows what. Wild boar, we're out in the boonies. All of a sudden, I see this shadow move over my left, and it scared the crap out of me; I almost jumped out of the train. And I look over, and it's Michael. He walked up the side of these coaches. It's not like a walkway you can walk on; he had to hang on. ... I don't know how he got over ... but he's in the cab with me, and he knows he's scared the crap out of me, and he's just laughing, and all he wanted me to do is turn the music up. My heart's pounding, I looked at him, and I said, "Don't do that!" ... I thought a bear or something was jumping in the cabin. He looked at me like a kid that got in trouble; he looked at me and goes, "Can you turn the music up a little bit?"[106]

Though Michael loved the ranch, he spent only sporadic time on the property until the latter years of his life. He spent much of his time traveling for work or in a condo in Los Angeles, close to recording studios. Friend David Nordahl recalled visiting Michael's condo for the first time in 1989 and how shocked he was by what he saw:

The man lived so simply. ... Two-bedroom apartment, small; you couldn't get in the kitchen because there was a piano shoved in the opening going into the kitchen. The second bedroom was all piled full of stuff, just memorabilia crap, nothing important, just thrown in there. And in the living room, there was a couch and a chair, a nice TV, and a nice sound system, of course, and a popcorn machine. Other than those things, you couldn't have gotten $50 for his furniture at a garage sale. He lived so simply. There's no cook. There's no maid. ... It was kind of like a teenage boy's room. Not decorated or anything. ... I was so surprised at that. ... I was just so impressed at how simply he lived. ... Now, the way he lived changed as soon as he got the kids because he was so concerned about their safety.

Nordahl also stated that Michael dressed as simply as he lived.[107] When Michael was asked why he never wore jewelry, he replied, "If I had it on, I would probably give it away to the first kid that walked up to me and said, 'Wow, I like your necklace.' Here, you can have it."[108] According to studio engineer CJ de Villar, Michael often came into the studio wearing "wrinkled, dirty clothes." One day, the singer Brandy arrived at the studio unannounced, wanting to meet Michael, and Michael told de Villar, "But I'm so stinky! I'm not dressed up, I'm a mess!"[109]

When asked how often Michael was at the ranch, Big Al responded, "The first several years, he would show up at the ranch sometimes just for a weekend or a week, several times a year. Obviously, when he was on tour, he didn't. But usually, when the tour took a break, he would come and spend at least a week there. Towards the end … he was there quite a bit more often."[110]

Despite spending little time on the property until later years, Michael put his heart and soul into Neverland. It was serene, peaceful, and idyllic, with lakes, beautiful trees, and rolling hills. Musical collaborator Brad Buxer called it "a magical place."[111] Michael himself called it "a serene and tranquil place to just relax and enjoy yourself and leave your troubled mind and things that irritate you in your heart and in your soul behind. Once you're into the gates, you are in a very wonderful, quiet, loving place. There are lakes and rolling hills and grass and trees, rides, and trains, a movie theater."[112]

Because Michael was rarely at Neverland in its early years, Big Al assumed he would have a very easy job when the ranch hired him. He recalled:

> It's kinda funny … when I made the deal to go to work there, I'm thinking, "How boring is this going to be?" … At that time, I didn't have a clue as to what all went on there, and I just was thinking, here's this guy that's got a lot of money, and he has an amusement park in his backyard. I had no idea about the groups that came in there and what all went on. I just thought we were sitting around

waiting for Michael to come home. And when he was on tour for eighteen months, we were going to have a lot of time to do whatever we wanted to do. Well, it didn't turn out that way.[113]

What groups was Big Al referring to? Unbeknownst to many, Neverland was essentially a full-time charity operation. Nine months out of the year, March through November, the ranch would invite groups of inner-city or terminally ill children to spend the day at Neverland. It would arrange these visits with schools in the Los Angeles area and various local charities. The ranch would host one to three visits a week, with an average of one hundred to two hundred guests per visit. In the three winter months, December through February, it would host fewer outings, perhaps one or two a month. The invited groups would arrive in the morning and enjoy the various facilities, including the arcade, movie theater, amusement park, and zoo. There would be a big barbecue lunch with more activities afterward. The kids would stay until four or five in the afternoon and then head home with souvenir bags filled with various items from the ranch.[114] Since many of the children who visited the ranch were very ill, the ranch was designed to cater to those with physical disabilities. The movie theater had several adjustable hospital beds,[115] wheelchair ramps were installed in every place that had stairs, and the carousel and steam train were also wheelchair accessible and had wheelchair locks. Big Al expressed, "We tried to make everything as accessible as we possibly could."[116] According to friend David Nordahl, "The guys that ran the rides, they went to Kansas City every six months and took special training to be able to extricate physically challenged children."[117]

For Big Al, one of the most memorable groups to visit was a group of burned children. He shared that the children were so severely burned that they looked like aliens. Their adult chaperones shared how meaningful that day was for the children. It was a rare opportunity for the children to be themselves and enjoy the facilities without having everyone stare at them.[118]

It was not only groups of children that enjoyed the ranch. Sometimes, elderly groups would be invited for the day as well. Violet Gaitan recalled one visit by an Alzheimer's group:

> Seeing these senior citizens, very elderly people, have a good time and just indulge … just taking in all the beauty, I think they knew they were safe, and they were with familiar people, perhaps not being confined into a space, you could see the relief on them. I think it meant a lot to them. … You could tell they were so relaxed, and they so enjoyed being out there. … Being there is very healing. … The beauty of being there is the peacefulness.[119]

Events were less frequent in the winter because Michael wanted to avoid having visitors look forward to the day and end up disappointed by a last-minute cancellation due to rain, which is frequent in the winter months. Big Al explained, "Some of these kids … have been dealing with disappointment all their life; we didn't want to add one more to them."[120]

Big Al said the events were a huge undertaking but well worth it. Any child invited onto the ranch as part of these groups could bring their siblings and parents. "We would get these letters—I mean letters and letters, three-ring binders full of letters—from the families of how important that day was; it was the most important day of their life. … The impact it had on people's lives is just unbelievable."[121] He described the letters as "heart-wrenching."[122] He recalled a touching moment, sitting at the ranch next to one of the young visitors who was not a fan of Michael's music. Big Al stated that the young visitor was "looking around, and I can tell he's really thinking about something, and he goes, 'You know, I don't know if I like Michael Jackson, the entertainer, but I know I would like Michael Jackson, the person.' That really hit me. … I was so blessed to be a part of it. I was just doing my job, but it was a very rewarding job."[123]

The events at the ranch meant a lot to Michael, even though he very rarely made an appearance at them. During an interview, Michael once expressed why he felt so much empathy for children who were ill or suffering—essentially forced to enter an adult world with adult stress at far too young an age, never knowing what it is like to experience the innocence of childhood: "I never had that chance too, as a child, so I knew what it felt like in that way, not being sick, but not having had a childhood. So, my heart goes out to those children."[124] Big Al noted about Michael:

> I could tell in his eyes and his voice how important Neverland was to him, not for him and his family and his friends, but for days like what I just described [event days]. ... That's what he built that place for, and that's what it was all about. ... It was really built to touch people's lives in a positive way that would last them forever. ... It was such a passion of his to have that and what we did for all those kids. His idea was for that to last forever, past him and I.[125]

Many often questioned Michael's childlike qualities. He was asked once during an interview, "Do you ever think that this is silly to have the llamas and the little choo choo train?" He responded:

> It's calling God silly to do that because God made all things, great and small, so that would be wrong. ... Other men have their Ferraris or an airplane or a helicopter or wherever they find their bliss, and my bliss is in giving and sharing and having simple, innocent fun. ... I've traveled the world ... and there are so many children in the cities who have never seen the mountains, who haven't been on a carousel, who haven't petted a horse or a llama, who've never seen them. ... I feel like I've won God's smile of approval because I'm doing something that brings joy and happiness to other people.[126]

David Nordahl proclaimed, "People that reach that level of fame and wealth ... the tendency is for people to kind of isolate themselves from the unpleasant parts of life, the people who are sick, the people who are poor, people who are hungry, people who are downtrodden, they tend to elevate themselves above that, so they don't have to see it. Michael saw it every day."[127]

Regarding the zoo on the property, Michael stated, "Many people made fun of me with my animals. If I come home from a hard day at the studio, and I come home to my deer or my chimps, and I can hug them, and they don't ask you for anything, they don't complain, they don't gossip, they just want a hug and some love."[128]

David Nordahl expressed similar sentiments:

> Michael grew up in a paranoid world. Anytime you're a money machine, everybody wants their mitts on it. They all want part of what you're making. And so, you never know who your friends are. He would refer to the people in the music industry as weasels and crooks ... because he'd been dealing with these people all the time. And that's the reason he loved animals so much because the animals' love was unconditional. ... They were a big comfort to Michael. He understood that children and animals are a lot alike; they offer unconditional love. They don't care if your clothes are tattered, if you're ugly, or if you're old or whatever; they still love you. When an animal loves you, you know it's genuine.[129]

Big Al said he would get "burned up" when people would say that Neverland was a trap for kids:[130]

> The whole time we operated Neverland people did not have a clue ... and I didn't know when I went to work there ... then I find out all the stuff we do, and he absolutely did not do it for the publicity. ... There were times in his career when ... his marketing people said we got to come out there and we got to publicize this, and I remember hearing him saying you're not going to use this place

or those kids to promote me, figure something else out. And I got to tell you, if I was in the position he's in, I'd have said go for it. ... And that just really told me that he absolutely did that 100 percent out of the kindness of his heart.[131]

Big Al described Michael as "generous," "compassionate," "caring," and "honest."[132] Violet Gaitan described him as "thoughtful and caring."[133] Big Al proclaimed, "[Michael] was a pretty amazing person to be around, and I did have a ton of respect for him."[134] Like so many who knew Michael, Big Al claimed that the image portrayed by the media did not match the person he knew: "I can tell you for a fact that if you spent five minutes with him, you would come away with a totally different view. ... He was about as down-to-earth, genuine, sincere a person as I've ever met in my life. ... Very down to earth, very sincere, very compassionate."[135]

Big Al referred to working at Neverland as "paradise." He divulged how he and Michael greeted each other. "He always asked me, 'Big Al, how are you doing?' And I always said, 'Just another day in paradise.' And he always laughed, and he always thought that was cool." He said Michael was always thoughtful. He recounted a time in the early 1990s when he [Big Al] had hurt his knee, and Michael called while out of town working:

> I haven't seen him in six, maybe eight months, and he goes, "How's your knee?" and I'm like looking around, "What is he talking about?" and I was kind of silent for a minute ... and he goes ... "Your knee, how's your knee?" ... And the tone of my voice gave it away that I didn't have a clue what he was talking about, and he said, "Big Al, last time I saw you, you were on crutches." ... And I thought to myself, "This guy remembered that?" It just blew me away that he remembered that and remembered to ask me. .... To me, it meant a lot. ... He cares about everybody.[136]

Indeed, Michael was pleasant to all the staff that worked at the ranch. Big

Al revealed, "He was extremely easy to work for ... he treated everybody great. ... People would be planting the flowers or mowing the grass or whatever, and he would stop and talk to them and thank them. He was nice to everybody."[137]

In addition to all the scheduled events for which Michael opened up his ranch to others, he invited onto the property tourists and fans who would sit by his gates. Fan Talitha Linehan recounted how she and some friends had been sitting outside the Neverland gates, and when Michael came out on his way out of town, he invited them onto the property and told his staff to treat them like royalty. "They treated us like princesses. ... It was amazing. ... Everyone was so nice to us," gushed Linehan.[138] Indeed, Michael was overly generous from a young age. When he was little, he used his allowance to buy candy and set up a store, but he "sold" the candy for free. His father told him that is not how business works. You are supposed to sell things for a profit, not a loss.[139]

Michael's charity work, including the charity work done at the ranch, was virtually unknown to the public. While touring, he visited many orphanages and children's hospitals without fanfare. One of these visits was to a Christmas party for orphans in Manila, Philippines. The lady in charge of the party warmly recounted Michael's visit, "He would patiently talk to the kids, one by one. ... He made sure it was meaningful."[140] In 2000, the *Guinness Book of World Records* listed him as the pop star to donate to the most charities. It is estimated he gave over $300 million to these various charities over the course of his lifetime.[141] His humanitarian work is essentially unknown due to his lack of advertising it. Friend David Nordahl shared:

> He was terribly modest. He really was. And the amazing thing is he never changed. I met him when he was at his peak. ... He was really at his peak. I've been around other Hollywood people, but success does something to them. They kind of change. They are not so thoughtful anymore. They're much more narcissistic.

And they love to give money to charities if they can get some TV time out of it. Or their tax person will say, "Listen, we need to invest some money in some charities here." But Michael was just the opposite. He would get upset if anybody would say something about something good that he did. I remember when I'd first met him, he'd given a check for, I think, $700,000 to the NAACP, and they wanted him to appear to present the check, and he absolutely refused. So, they went and talked to Liz Taylor, and she finally got him to do that, and he was absolutely crushed. He told me, "If you do a charitable act, and then you go tell people about it, then it's not about what you did; it's about you. So, then, it means nothing." … He never changed. He didn't get a big head. He didn't become narcissistic.[142]

Doctor Patrick Treacy shared:

Because he was such a good and gentle person and because he did it in a total Christian way, he never really got the credit for it. … People were unaware of his humanitarian work or the depth of it. At times, Michael lived penniless, and I know this, and he still would be giving away and had given away many, many millions to people he would see as less fortunate.[143]

Michael taught other young stars to follow his lead. Actress Jennifer Love Hewitt recounted the lessons Michael taught her when they filmed a commercial together when she was just ten years old:

We spent the whole day together. We were dancing together. He taught me how to do some of his go-up-on-the-toes thing. … It was amazing. … Here's what I loved about him most: is [sic] at the end of the day, I had to go to this charity function, and … he was like, "You don't know how important it is that you are doing something that is special and important for other people," and he was like, "Never lose that, always be that person." And I was like, ok, yes sir, absolutely. And he wrote a very big donation to this charity function that I was going to that night and sent a check in my name on my behalf, which is not something that I would have been able to do at the time, and sent it just to sort of button how important it is to give to other people ... and I just thought that was extraordinary. ... And then I got to go to Neverland Ranch. ... My mom and I went a few times.[144]

Michael's hair stylist, Carol LaMere, shared similar sentiments: "There are things about [Michael] people didn't even know. ... He never called the press to tell them what he did."[145] Michael's nephew, Taj Jackson, said his uncle taught him that "the biggest charity you can give is when people don't even know it's coming from you. ... He felt like if you're doing it to get recognition, then you weren't really doing it for the purity of it."[146]

Michael instilled the same values in his children. His eldest son, Prince, created the Heal Los Angeles non-profit with a college friend of his, John Muto, who was inspired by Michael's music. The non-profit is named after Michael's song "Heal the World." It focuses on education and healthy living for inner-city youth and families and offers cooking and fitness classes. Prince spoke of how his father influenced the work done by the Heal Los Angeles foundation:

> When you do philanthropic work ... you tend to carry the weight or the struggles of the people that you're trying to help, and that's really when I hear my father's voice the most is [sic] because those are the times you struggle the most and you almost wonder *How can I continue to do this?* It's during those moments that I hear him: "Somebody has to do it. You have to do it. You have to keep pushing forward, and it's important that we do this." He's kind of always on my shoulder, in my ear, motivating me to keep that moral compass pointing north.[147]

6

Michael's Voice

As time went on, Michael matured. While his writing started with songs that were fun to create and sing, he later developed material that had a much deeper meaning. His need to have a voice that reflected humanity became more pronounced. The emotions in his songs reached a greater depth and touched more people around the world. - Sound engineer Matt Forger[148]

Michael gave comfort to others not only through his ranch, time, and money but also through his music. After the *Bad* album release, Michael released his next album, *Dangerous*, on November 26, 1991. With this release, his music continued to grow in depth.

The first song released off the album was the anthem "Black or White." It soared to the number one spot on the charts and remained there for six weeks.[149] It was a fun, upbeat song, with the chorus professing that it did not matter if one was black or white. While the general tone of the song was cheerful, it also displayed a sense of frustration. Michael angrily sang of how tired he was of seeing people mistreated.

In a rap section spoken by collaborator Bill Bottrell, the song expresses how influential forces keep a divided and unjust society in place by offering unfair protection for the crimes of the powerful and causing grief for the rest of humanity. It refers to imperialism as a global war over territory. The song also alludes to the fact that we are only given the perspective of the dominant side in these global conflicts.

The music video accompanying the song was the most controversial video released by Michael up to that point, creating much backlash. The video opens by zooming in from space down to Earth. It lands in the home of a typical suburban family. The child is upstairs listening to music. The mother reads gossip magazines downstairs, and the father watches sports. The three are utterly oblivious to each other, lost in their own worlds, until the father finally yells at the son to turn down his music. The intro conveys the isolation and apathy of the typical suburban home. The mother and father are preoccupied with a distraction—gossip magazines and sports—blind to the struggles of the outside world. As the song begins, the video transitions to a utopian version of the world. It shows Michael moving from one continent and culture to another, seamlessly joining native dancers as he traverses the planet. He begins in Africa, then Thailand, followed by dances with Native Americans, then an Indian lady, after which he travels to Russia. The utopian section of the video ends with various individuals across many ethnicities singing the end of the song. It displays one individual at a time and then uses technology to morph that person into the next. As the section ends, the camera pulls away, and it becomes clear that what was just seen was not reality but rather a film set. The music has ended, but the video has not.

It then shows a black panther walking off the set into the night and morphing into Michael Jackson. The most controversial part of the video begins. Michael enters a ghetto and begins to dance. The movement is a display of frustration and rage. It is quite explicit, with multiple crotch grabs, and ultimately turns violent as the audience sees windows smashed. Michael then falls into a puddle of water, screaming in frustration, but no one is there to hear him. Soon afterward, he converts back into a black panther. As the panther walks away, the camera zooms out, and it becomes clear to the viewing audience that the panther in the ghetto is being watched through a TV screen. It is Bart Simpson who is watching the TV. His father, Homer Simpson, comes into the room and yells at Bart to "turn off that noise," after which Homer shuts off the TV, and the video ends with nothing but static.

The meaning of the video is open to interpretation, but it does convey that perhaps what is blocking the utopia in the middle of the video from being reached is apathy toward those who are suffering. It opens with the typical suburban home, distracted by gossip and sports, utterly ignorant of the pains of others, and ends with a typical suburban home essentially shutting its eyes to the display of that pain. The censoring and shutting off of the TV at the end of the music video was a premonition, as the panther dance sequence was censored from all future broadcasts of the video. Michael responded to the controversy: "Anger and rage are the prelude to a shift in consciousness. Unless we feel rage at some of the inequities and injustices of our society, there is no hope for transformation."[150]

The choice to use a black panther in the dance sequence was likely not coincidental. In their historical analysis of the Black Panther Party, founded in 1966, authors Joshua Bloom and Waldo E. Martin Jr. wrote that the founding members "declared themselves part of the global revolution against American imperialism."[151] The authors said of the Black Panthers:

> With an unpopular imperial war underway in Vietnam, popular anti-imperialist movements agitating internationally, and a crisis of legitimacy brewing in the Democratic Party, they posited a single worldwide struggle against imperialism encompassing Vietnamese resistance against the United States, draft resistance against military service, and their own struggle to liberate the black community. In the face of brutal repression, the Black Panther Party forged powerful alliances, drawing widespread support not only from moderate blacks but also from many nonblacks, as well as from anti-imperialist governments and movements around the

globe.[152]

Michael expressed similar sentiments in the song "Jam." He wrote of how people are not willing even to assist a neighbor and that society is "conditioned" to ignore the cries of others.

Michael's favorite song on the album was "Heal the World." In later years, he was asked if he could only perform one song for the rest of his life, what would it be? Michael first replied by asking if he could pick two or three. Then the song he mentioned first was "Heal the World."[153] He elaborated that a song needs to have a message that is "immortal, that can relate to any time and space." The song urged all to aim for a more beautiful, kind, and peaceful world and to reflect the goodness of God's creation. He also called for the nations to disarm.

As with the song "Man in the Mirror," Michael did not appear in the music video for "Heal the World." Instead, he displayed children playing in various regions across the globe—from Asia to Africa to Israel and Palestine—as soldiers with guns stood nearby. After watching the children interact without prejudice, ultimately, the soldiers laid down their weapons.

Michael's music was growing more and more meaningful. He wrote a lot of music and poetry during this era, much of which was never publicly released. He did not shy away from controversial topics. In one song, written in the late 1980s, he sang about abortion, referring to it as being against the sanctity of human life, which he believed to be made in the image of God. The song was ultimately released after his death. In another, written in 1993 but not known ever to be recorded, he wrote about Palestine. Titling it "Palestine, Don't Cry," he spoke of how the peace that existed just a century prior has since been replaced with endless war and suffering. He shared his prayers and expressed his heartfelt commitment to the afflicted region.[154] He released an entire book of songs and poetry in July of 1992 entitled *Dancing the Dream*. One poem included in that book was "Planet Earth." Michael's estate released a previously recorded spoken version after his passing. The poem was essentially a love song to nature.

In another poem, titled "Mother Earth," Michael talked about the deep nurturing relationship humans should have with nature but often do not. He reminded his readers that the earth is a "living, nurturing being" that needs to be taken care of if we expect her to care for us in return.

Both through Neverland and Michael's music and poetry, it is clear he had a deep connection to nature. He shared in a 2005 interview, "I'm a great believer in holistic, natural foods, and … herbs … God's medicine, instead of Western chemicals."[155] Studio engineer Matt Forger said of Michael, "He was always in awe of the beauty of nature."[156]

While Michael continued to make his fair share of fun songs during this era, there is no doubt his music had become more profound.

7

The Music and the Dance

When I create my music, I feel like an instrument of nature. - Michael Jackson[157]

It was Michael's connection to nature that inspired him to write some of his most famous music. He wrote many songs in what he referred to as his "giving tree" at Neverland. He revealed, "It inspires me. ... I climb up high, and I look down on its branches, and it gives me so many ideas. I've written so many of my songs in this tree." Some of those songs included "Heal the World," "Will You Be There," "Black or White," and "Childhood."[158]

Jimmy Van Norman, a bodyguard for Michael, recounted how he once witnessed Michael working in his "giving tree":

> He didn't see me, and he was up in a tree, and I was like amazed because I'm hearing all these noises coming from this tree and I look up, and it's him. It was amazing watching him create. He was always creating. I had the room next to him [at hotels], so 3 a.m. ... I'm hearing the piano going or the music blasting. He's creating, and I'm going, "I got to get to sleep."[159]

Big Al stated that when Michael was in the tree, he was usually reading something or writing in a book. The tree was where Michael sat "for peace and quiet and meditation and maybe being creative and writing a song."[160] Michael said that what inspired him most was nature, animals, and children—in essence, creation. "I think the majority of my success is from these sources. … You just play off of life," he proclaimed in one interview.[161]

Michael also believed strongly that music should be universal. He once said, "I don't believe in stylizing or branding any type of music. I think a great artist should be able to just create any style, any form … from rock to pop to folk to gospel to spiritual to just wonderful music where anybody can sing it, from the Irish farmer to a lady who scrubs toilets in Harlem."[162] Keyboardist Rory Kaplan said when he would look out at the crowds during a concert, he would see everyone from two-year-olds to grandmothers. He said Michael had a much more diverse audience than most performers. Kaplan explained, "He was so welcoming. … Michael touched everyone's hearts. … He just touched everybody in that sort of heartfelt way."[163] Michael felt music should offer people "a sense of escapism in time of need" and give them "love" and "bliss."[164]

Many who have asked Michael how he wrote his music were often left frustrated with his vague replies. They wanted more details than he offered. He explained in an interview:

> The songwriting process is something very difficult to explain because it's very spiritual. You're really just in the hands of God. It's as if it's been written already … in its entirety, before you were born. You're really the source through which the song comes. They just fall right into your lap. … You don't have to do much thinking about it. And I feel guilty having to put my name sometimes on the songs. I do write them. I compose them. I write them. I do the scoring. I do the lyrics. I do the melodies. But still, it's the work of God.[165]

In another interview, he stated, "Every song is different. Sometimes, it

49

happens quickly; sometimes, it happens slowly. No one can quite say what the creative process is because I have nothing to do with it almost. It's created in space. It's God's work, not mine."[166] He explained, "You can't teach it, it has to come from inside; it's a gift."[167]

Talent can be difficult to explain when it comes so effortlessly. Michael would not schedule specific writing sessions; instead, he allowed ideas to flow naturally. He explained, "If I sat here and said, 'Right, I'm going to write the best song I've ever written,' nothing happens. Nowadays, artists seem to get in the way of the music. Get out of the way of the music! Let the music write itself." Michael said ideas would come to him in the most random places at the most random times of the day.[168]

Despite the difficulty of explaining talent, we do have some insight into how Michael created his music. He once tried to break down the creative process:

> Usually, when I write songs, I vocally … [sing] melody into a tape recorder. … I'll have a tape recorder, and I'll just sing the bass part into the tape recorder. … [And then I] put the chords of the melody over the bass lick. And that's what inspires the melody or the other sounds that I'm hearing in my head. … And the lyrics, the strings, the chords, everything comes at that moment like a gift that is put right into your head.[169]

Even though Michael did not play any instruments or read or write sheet music, he would communicate with his voice what he wanted from the musicians working with him.[170] Beatboxing involves imitating the sound of instruments with the voice. Musical collaborator Brad Buxer explained how he and Michael worked:

> He would just beatbox, and I'd take the beatbox and chop it up and put it in a sampler and do drums around that. These would be his ideas, but I would execute the idea in the most intuitive way.

So, he wouldn't have to say, "I want this beat there;" he would just sing something. As he's beatboxing, he's saying, "I want the strings doing this." It wouldn't make any sense to most people.[171]

Vocal director and assistant musical director Kevin Dorsey summed up, "Even though Michael was not a musician, he wrote with his mouth and his voice, if you will."[172] Collaborator Bill Bottrell stated about Michael, "He can convey it [a song arrangement] with his voice like nobody. Not just singing the song's lyrics, but he can convey a feeling in a drum part or a synthesizer part. He's really good at conveying those things."[173] Buxer called Michael a "musical genius."[174]

Another collaborator, studio engineer Rob Hoffman, broke down how Michael would use the same tools available to others but would arrange them in a way that no one else could. A song loop is a section of music that repeats itself for an indefinite period of time. Michael took a set of loops off a widely available CD that anyone could get and used it to create one of his songs. Hoffman explained:

They were all laid out on a keyboard, and he sat with Brad, and he said, "This loop goes here, and that loop goes there, and then you're going to layer a snare drum on top of this." The way Michael used almost the same tools that everyone else had available to them … is amazing because you'll hear those sounds other places. … It's almost like giving an expert chef your kitchen, and he cooks a meal out of your kitchen that you could never dream of, and you're like, "But that's my kitchen, it's my pots and pans, and my spices, but it's still better than anything else I could have cooked." … It was a lesson; wow, Michael Jackson took the most commercially available, probably the biggest selling sample CD of all time at that moment, used those same sounds that everybody else is using, and came up with a song that's ten times better than anybody else ever did. How did he do that? That was a good lesson. It's not the spices,

... it's not the sounds that everybody else has, it's how he layered them, how he used them. ... He was a musical genius.[175]

Bodyguard Bill Whitfield expressed, "We all use the [term] ... musical genius, but I think we use it lightly. He was a musical genius, a musical wizard because there were times in which he would play music and he would ask us ... 'You hear that, you hear that?' and we'd be like, 'No.' ... We did not hear it. Honestly, we did not hear what he was hearing."[176]

Michael was also known to have high expectations of the people he worked with. Buxer called him a "workaholic" and "perfectionist."[177] Michael once shared, "I've had musicians who really get angry with me because I'll make them do something literally several hundred to a thousand times until it's what I want it to be. But then afterward, they'll call me back on the phone, and they'll apologize and say, 'You were absolutely right. I've never played better. I've never done better work. I outdid myself.'"[178]

Sound engineer Matt Forger discussed the dedication Michael put into his music:

> The thing that most dramatically struck me was his degree of professionalism and his dedication to the music. ... When it came to the music, he was absolutely dead serious; he was totally focused on the music, to the smallest detail, and ... he knew exactly what something should be, how something should sound, how the interplay between the instruments or the percussion or something vocally ... should sound. ... He knew exactly what to do to get the sound that he wanted.[179]

Just as with music, Michael was also a natural dancer. Choreographer Vincent Paterson spoke of Michael's talent as a dancer:

> He just had this unbelievable electricity ... that just flowed, shot off

his body, and you sort of were zapped by it if you were anywhere near it. ... He was not a trained dancer. He didn't take jazz and ballet and all of those things that the rest of us who surrounded him did. ... But if you look at him and you look at us, there's no difference. It's as if he has trained every single day for twenty-five years, like anybody else did. Phenomenal, just phenomenal. ... Everybody was shocked beyond belief.[180]

As with music, Michael felt dance was connected to a higher source. He explained:

People want to dance. It's part of the human condition. It's part of our biological makeup; our cells dance when we hear beats, a one-year-old child will start moving hearing music. How do they know to move? Because it's biological. It's not just hearing of the ears; it's feeling and playing music. The grass, the trees, and the flowers, they are all influenced by music. They become more beautiful and more vibrant in how they grow. Music is a very important and powerful substance, and all the planets in the universe make music. It's called music of the spheres. They all make a different note. They make harmony.[181]

Michael felt the artist should allow the music to drive the dance. He explained, "I don't create the dance. The dance creates itself. ... Dancing is about interpretation. You become the accompaniment of the music."[182] He said he would watch dancers, and he could see they were not doing it right. He conveyed:

You can tell right away when an artist, you can read it on her face when she's dancing, she's counting, one and two and three and four and five and six and seven. ... That's the wrong concept with dance. Dancing is about feeling, not about thinking, so when they count, they're thinking. ... [You have to] become the bass, become the drums, become the guitar, the strings, you [have to] just become a oneness.[183]

Michael had a deep spiritual connection to music and art. And while he worked very hard at it, he let it flow naturally and did not force it. He was an artist in the truest sense. As he said, he was an instrument of nature. He let God and nature express their creativity through him.

8

1993

If I go through with this, I win big time. There's no way that I lose. I've checked that out inside out. ... I get everything I want, and ... Michael's career will be over.
- Evan Chandler

At the start of 1993, Michael Jackson was on top of the world. Yes, the press had been increasingly harsh toward him since the mid-1980s, but he was still mega-successful with one number-one song after another. He had just finished the first leg of a global tour promoting his latest album and donated the entire proceeds to charity. In the fall of 1992, the Bucharest concert of his *Dangerous* tour aired on HBO and received massive ratings. In early 1993, Michael performed at the Super Bowl. It became the first time that ratings increased from the first half to the second half of the game, as the halftime show drew in a global audience, one typically not interested in American football.[184] In early February 1993, Michael sat down for a live interview with Oprah Winfrey, which garnered a record-breaking viewership of 90 million. On February 24, 1993, he received the Grammy Legend Award at the Thirty-Fifth Annual Grammy Awards. During his acceptance speech, he spoke of his love for children:

> Many of our world's problems today—from the inner-city crimes
> to large-scale wars and terrorism and our overcrowded prisons—

are a result of the fact that children have had their childhoods stolen from them. The magic, the wonder, the mystery, and the innocence of a child's heart are the seeds of creativity that will heal the world. ... What we need to learn from children is not childish. Being with them connects us to the deeper wisdom of life. ... They know the solutions that lie waiting to be recognized within our own hearts. Today, I would like to thank all the children of the world, including the sick and deprived—I am so sensitive to your pain.[185]

It seemed as if the world was Michael's oyster. He was creating beautiful music, selling out concerts, garnering massive platforms, and using those platforms to spread messages he cared about. But it would soon all come crashing down. Michael had withstood many attacks up to this point. But the next one would forever alter his life.

In August 1993, the press broke a story alleging Michael Jackson had molested a young boy. To fully assess the claim's veracity, it is vital to take a step back and review the events that led to the allegation. The man who set in motion the allegations was Evan Chandler. His original name was Evan Robert Charmatz. He married June Wong, an attractive lady with a European and Asian background who briefly worked as a model. They had a son named Jordan Chandler in 1980.[186] In 1985, June and Evan divorced, and June married a man named David Schwartz that same year. June and David had a daughter named Lily.[187] According to a family friend, June divorced Evan at least partly due to his "temper." The court awarded June sole custody of Jordan and ordered Evan to pay $500 a month in child support. By 1993, Evan owed his ex-wife $68,000 in unpaid child support.[188] June separated from her second husband, David, in August of 1992 and officially divorced him in 1994.[189]

In May 1992, a few months before June's separation from David, Michael Jackson's vehicle broke down on a busy Los Angeles street about a mile from David's car rental business, Rent-A-Wreck. The wife of Mel Green, an employee at Rent-A-Wreck, spotted Michael's car. When David Schwartz heard Green was bringing Michael down to Rent-A-Wreck, he phoned his wife, June, and asked her to come down with Jordan and Lily to meet Michael. Jordan was a big fan of Michael's, and upon meeting him, June informed Michael that Jordan had mailed him a drawing after the singer's hair caught on fire in 1984. June gave Michael the family's phone number and suggested he call Jordan. Green stated, "It was almost as if she was forcing the boy on him. I think Michael felt he owed the boy something, and that's when it all started."[190] That first meeting lasted approximately five to ten minutes.[191]

During this stage of his life, Michael was friends with many children Jordan's age, some of the closest and most well-known being actor Macaulay Culkin, who later became godfather to Michael's children, and Brett Barnes, who stayed close to Michael until the end of Michael's life. To this day, both defend Michael's innocence. Barnes stated in 2022, "I could never see [Michael] doing anything bad to another human being, let alone a child."[192] It is important to keep in mind that Michael had a very abnormal upbringing and may have had some arrested development in various aspects of his life. Now, for the first time in his life he was being given opportunities to have genuine friendships instead of just working around the clock. He likely found something in these friendships that he had missed in his youth.

Susan Blond, an executive at Epic Records, recalled fondly what Michael was like when he was eighteen years old, "Here he was, having hits already, and having this genius brain, but as a person, he was [still] like a child. He would take my pocketbook, turn it upside-down, and everything would fall out. ... You'd expect a four-year-old to do that."[193]

Sound engineer Brad Sundberg referred to Michael's mid-1990s relationship with Lisa Marie Presley as "Two junior-highers in love ... laughing like two seventh graders, probably like I would have done with my first crush, and it was real. ... Lisa was probably more mature than Michael, but it just worked at that time. It was as real as I guess you would say [for] two junior highers that were deeply in love and they're going to spend the rest of their lives together, but it doesn't quite work out that way."[194]

Sundberg, who, in addition to working on Michael's music, often worked at Neverland installing sound equipment for Michael, further stated:

> I spent years at that ranch. Michael asked me to build him music systems and lighting systems and control systems ... so I have been in bathrooms, bedrooms, under beds, in closets, in upstairs little rooms, and different things. ... There was nothing, there was nothing that I ever saw that was the least bit, "Oh boy, I'm not sure about that." ... He was a kid; he was a big kid. ... There just isn't a cell in my body that believes that he could turn a fun afternoon, a water balloon fight, into something monstrous and sexual. ... [He] was the antithesis of monstrous.

When asked if Michael was gay, Sundberg replied, "Not a chance."[195]

There are other reasons Michael may have found value in relationships with younger people at this point in his life. When he was a child, adults constantly surrounded him. Many of them mentored him. As such, he may have wanted to pay it forward and mentor the next generation. And contrary to the public narrative, Michael was not just friends with boys but also girls. Actress Kelley Parker, who starred in Michael's 1988 film *Moonwalker*, talked about the influence Michael had on her:

> He was always pushing me to be better and teaching me about the artistic process. To have someone of his creative genius take the time to teach you at the age of ten is like getting the winning lotto ticket. ... Michael never once treated me as a kid, always as an equal.[196] ... He is intertwined in all of who I am. I became a dancer because of him. I became an artist because he inspired

me to dream and a writer because he taught me the power of moving people through words and actions.[197] ... I have nothing but amazing memories from the entire time that I knew him and was friends with him. I can't say enough good things. He just had this unconditional love. He was so pure.[198]

Like Culkin and Barnes, Parker spent time at Neverland, remained friends with Michael for many years, and last saw him a few weeks before his death.[199]

The media made a big deal about kids staying overnight at Neverland, but those who have stayed at the ranch have always maintained that it was innocent fun. Studio engineer Brad Sundberg explained:

When you went to Neverland, you didn't want to leave. It was the most fun place you can imagine. ... Even if I was up there, I might be working on something, and Michael would be there, and it would be Macaulay or something, and they won't leave. I know it sounds awkward, but my perception is, yeah, we had a cool TV in his bedroom, they go in there and watch a movie, and I know it sounds odd, but Michael would be like, "Ok, guys, I have to get some sleep, you guys have to go to bed," and they'd be like, "No, we want to stay here." Does it make any sense in the normal world? No. Do you take that leap to absolute deviant, monstrous behavior? I can't.[200]

Michael's ex-wife, Lisa Marie Presley, stated, "I've seen these children; they don't let him go to the bathroom without running in there with him. They won't let him out of their sight."[201]

Violet Gaitan, Michael's head of security at Neverland, shared similar sentiments: "I never had any concerns other than the kids kind of getting a little out of hand every once in a while. ... You have to remember there's more than one child. There are groups of kids. ... Parents were there. It wasn't a free-for-all." Gaitan laughed warmly as she recounted, "I actually saw a lot of times when Michael was exhausted from being with kids. ... It wasn't as though he was having this sort of inappropriate relationship or unbalanced relationship with them. ... He needed to get away from them at times. ... [But] they could not get enough of him."[202]

Evan Chandler worked as a dentist in Beverly Hills. Though he ran a successful business, he did have some issues in that career, including a ninety-day suspension and a two-and-a-half-year probation by the Board of Dental Examiners in the early 1980s for "gross ignorance and/or inefficiency." In the early 1990s, he was again sued for dental negligence, which was eventually settled out of court. Despite a relatively successful dental practice, Evan wanted to pursue a career as a Hollywood script writer. In 1992, he wrote the screenplay for the film *Robin Hood: Men in Tights*. Until Jordan met Michael, Evan had not shown much interest in his son. He was not paying his court-ordered child support. He had promised to buy Jordan a computer so that they could write screenplays together, but he never did. Evan, by the early 1990s, was re-married with two new young children.[203]

According to June, Michael called approximately one to two months after their initial meeting. He then called roughly once a month before he invited the family (June, Lily, and Jordan) up to Neverland in February 1993.[204] According to Michael's friend David Nordahl:

Ever since he was little, he never had any friends that were normal people. They were always people that were in the business. Because he was not free to just walk about or to play with neighbor kids or anything like that ... he was so vulnerable that when he met "normal" people like the extortionists from 1993 he was just so happy because these people befriended him. He ran out of gas in his Chevy Blazer at that intersection, and that lady and her boy ... helped him. And he was so happy that he had normal friends, and then they turned on him.[205]

According to June Chandler's attorney, Michael Freeman, once Evan saw that Jordan had befriended Michael, he began to take an interest in his son. Freeman stated, "My recollection was that he [Evan] was not very interested in Jordy prior to the time that Jordy took up with Michael, and as soon as Jordy took up with Michael, Evan became the most interested parent in the world."[206] Initially Evan bragged about the relationship to friends. He invited Michael to stay over at his house in May 1993, and Michael accepted. An investigative report in *GQ* alleged that Evan went as far as asking Michael to build him a new home with more space for visitors.[207] According to June Chandler's testimony, Michael also stayed over at her house in April and May of 1993 quite frequently.[208] In May 1993, Michael invited June and her two children to attend the World Music Awards with him in Europe. Freeman stated, "Evan began to get jealous of the involvement and felt left out." As a result, Evan became increasingly volatile.[209]

Due to Evan's erratic behavior, David Schwartz, June's separated husband, decided to record a phone conversation with Evan on July 8, 1993. At this time, Jordan had not made any allegations of Michael molesting him. The phone call was very revealing about Evan's frame of mind. He came off as jealous and angry that Michael and June were avoiding him. Indeed, Michael's disinterest in Evan seemed to be Evan's primary gripe. At one point in the conversation, Evan said, "I had a good communication with Michael. We were friends. I liked him. ... There was no reason why he had to stop calling me. He could have called me." While Evan did not explicitly state that he planned to accuse Michael of molesting his child, his desire to destroy Michael and June was evident. When David asked Evan why he did not like Michael, Evan replied, "Because he broke up my family, that's why ... I mean that to me was the worst thing anybody could do to me." This was an odd response, given Evan paid no attention to Jordan before Michael came into the picture. It is also notable that Evan said it was the worst thing anybody could do to *him*, not his family, implying a degree of narcissism on

Evan's part. Indeed, Evan stated, "I'm blaming all three of them [Michael, June, and Jordan]."

Evan also informed David of his planned revenge. He said he would like to see "everybody get destroyed like they've destroyed me." Evan stated that he had found an attorney:

> I picked the nastiest son of a bitch I could find, and all he wants to do is get this out in the public as fast as he can, as big as he can, and humiliate as many people as he can. ... I mean, it could be a massacre if I don't get what I want. ... Once I make that phone call, this guy's just going to destroy everybody in sight in any devious, nasty, cruel way that he can do it. And I've given him full authority to do that. ... If I go through with this, I win big time. There's no way that I lose. I've checked that out inside out. ... I get everything I want, and ... they will be totally destroyed forever. ... June is gonna lose Jordy. She will have no right to ever see him again. ... Michael's career will be over.

When David asked how this would affect Jordan, Evan responded, "That's irrelevant to me." But about Michael, Evan said, "This man is gonna be humiliated beyond belief. You'll not believe it. He will not believe what's going to happen to him—beyond his worst nightmares. He will not sell one more record. ... There are other people involved that are waiting for my phone call that are intentionally going to be in certain positions. ... Everything is going according to a certain plan that isn't just mine."[210]

David shared the taped phone conversation with June, and the next day, July 9, 1993, he and June shared the tape with Michael's private investigator, Anthony Pellicano. "After listening to the tape for ten minutes, I knew it was about extortion," claimed Pellicano. That same day, Pellicano met with Jordan and asked him "very pointed questions," including, "Has Michael ever touched you? Have you ever seen him naked in bed?" Jordan answered no to all of Pellicano's questions. He told Pellicano that Michael had never done anything bad to him and that his father just wanted money.[211]

On July 11, Evan asked June if Jordan could stay with him for a "one-week visitation period," and June obliged. Evan never returned Jordan to her.[212] Barry Rothman, the "nasty, son-of-a-bitch" attorney that Evan hired, phoned Beverly Hills psychiatrist Dr. Mathis Abrams. Rothman gave Abrams a hypothetical situation of a boy spending time with an adult male. In response, on July 15, Abrams sent Rothman a letter in which he stated that "reasonable suspicion would exist that sexual abuse may have occurred." Abrams also informed Rothman that if this were a real and not a hypothetical case, the law would require him to report the allegation to the Los Angeles County Department of Children's Services (DCS).[213]

Geraldine Hughes was a legal secretary working for Barry Rothman during this time. Although it was some time before she figured out the case had anything to do with Michael Jackson, she immediately noticed the unique way that Rothman was handling Chandler as a client. As such, she kept notes of the ongoing activity in her personal notebook. She stated of Evan Chandler:

> He would call Rothman's office almost daily. My antennas went up ... because usually, when someone would call, if Rothman was standing at my desk, he would just pick up the phone ... but whenever Chandler called, I noticed his whole demeanor was different. He would say, "Put him on hold." His office was all the way at the other end. He would walk all the way to the other end, go in his office, shut the door, and that's how he would take only Chandler's calls. ... Everybody else he was more casual with. ... He never told me this case had anything to do with Michael Jackson, and that's unusual because ... when you are dealing with anything high profile, you usually tell your staff because there is a higher level of confidentiality that goes with that, so you want

your staff to know let's be careful with this. ... I didn't know that case involved Michael until I was typing the actual declaration that had his name in it. ... I found it odd that after their many conversations, there were never any memos. ... At the least, there should have been documentation of calls [and meetings] for billing purposes. ... I don't remember doing bills for any of the phone calls [or meetings] that he had with Chandler. ... Not to have any sort of record ... that was unusual.[214]

In her notebook, dated July 27, Hughes scribbled, "Rothman wrote letter to Chandler advising him how to report child abuse without liability to parent."[215] This was no doubt based on the information Rothman received from Dr. Abrams, who informed him that if a psychiatrist knows of abuse, he is legally obligated to report it.

On August 4, 1993, Chandler met with Michael and his attorneys in a suite at the Westwood Marquis Hotel. Upon seeing Michael, Chandler hugged him. Michael's attorney, Bert Fields, recalled, "I was sitting in a conference room next to Michael, and the father came into the room and saw Michael and went quickly across the room, hugged him, and said, 'Michael, it's been so long since I've seen you,' which was just flabbergasting because here's a father claiming that this man had abused his son sexually and rushes across the room to hug him. Impossible."[216] Evan shared the letter from Dr. Abrams outlining the hypothetical scenario of abuse. According to Pellicano, Chandler pointed his finger at Michael after the meeting and warned, "I'm going to ruin you." That evening, Rothman and Chandler met with Pellicano in Rothman's office. They made their demand for a $20 million payout.[217] According to Michael's friend David Nordahl, the $20 million request came from Evan feeling snubbed over a film deal:

I was working on sketches for [Michael's] film production company called Lost Boys Productions ... and Sony had given him $40 million to start this production company and so that little boy's dad, who considered himself to be showbusiness material because he'd written part of a script ... after that, he considered himself a Hollywood screenwriter. And being friends with Michael, and his son being friends with Michael, and his former wife being friends with Michael, this guy had assumed that Michael was going to make him a partner in this film production company, and that's where the $20 million came from because he wanted half of that Sony money. ... Norma [Michael's assistant] told me about that before it ever hit the media. It was just another extortion attempt. Michael would get between fifty and sixty extortion attempts a year.[218]

On August 9, Pellicano returned to Rothman's office with a counteroffer of $1 million to fund three screenplays that Evan could work on with his son Jordan. These screenplays would allow Evan to reconnect with his son since Evan was complaining that Michael had stolen his son's time from him. Pellicano gave this offer only to make a record of the extortion attempt; he never intended to make a deal. When Rothman declined the offer, saying it was too low, Pellicano returned on August 13 with an even lower offer, $350,000 for just one script. After this, Rothman realized Pellicano was not serious about negotiating.[219]

By this point, Jordan had been away from his mother for almost a month. According to Evan, he administered the drug sodium amytal to Jordan as part of a dental procedure, and while under the drug, Jordan admitted to being molested. Evan likely made this claim because, at the time, the drug was purported to be a "truth serum," but it has since been uncovered that the drug makes one highly suggestible, essentially the opposite of a truth serum. Evan's claims that he administered the drug are dubious. He likely made the claim because he thought it bolstered the credibility of the accusation.

It is more likely that Jordan changed his initial story of not being molested due to pressure put on him by his father and Rothman after being separated from his mother. Rothman's legal assistant, Geraldine Hughes, claims to have seen Jordan in Rothman's office in what appeared to her to be a coaching session.[220]

Three days after Pellicano's reduced offer of $350,000, June Chandler's attorney, Michael Freeman, informed Rothman that he would be filing papers to force Evan to return Jordan to June. Evan then quickly reacted and took Jordan to Dr. Abrams, the same psychiatrist he had relied on the prior month to assess a hypothetical scenario. Jordan then disclosed to Dr. Abrams that Michael Jackson had molested him. He said there was only touching and no penetration. A medical exam could have verified penetration. By limiting the accusation to just touching, there would be no way to disprove it. As Abrams had previously explained to Rothman, the psychiatrist was then required to report the allegation to the Department of Children's Services, which he did.[221] They, in turn, notified the police. Did Evan send Jordan to the psychiatrist to avoid having to hand him back over to June? Had Jordan returned to his mother, would he have agreed to make allegations of molestation?

The local LA news station KNBC-TV broke the story on the afternoon of August 23. They stated a police warrant had been issued to search Michael's ranch and condominium. The story then spread like wildfire across the global media. A DCS employee illegally leaked a copy of the abuse report to the press with all of its salacious accusations.[222]

Rothman's legal assistant, Geraldine Hughes, was shocked when she heard the allegations. Up to that point, to her knowledge, all that was going on was a negotiation for a movie script. She said, "That came out of nowhere. ... I knew he was going to do something other than return the child [to his mother]." However, she never expected that something to be a molestation accusation.[223]

The following day, August 24, Michael kicked off the next leg of his world tour, performing in Thailand. His nephews Taj, TJ, and Taryll Jackson flew to Asia to be with him. Taj Jackson shared, "He was really adamant, he was like, 'They're not doing this to me. I know what they're trying to do.' ... He wanted to fight it."[224]

While June initially rejected Evan's claims of molestation, she came around after the police told her in late August 1993 that Michael fit the profile of a pedophile, even though he did not. According to sources close to June, she also feared what Evan and Rothman might do if she did not side with them. She worried they would accuse her of parental neglect. June's attorney, Michael Freeman, resigned. He stated, "The whole thing was such a mess. I felt uncomfortable with Evan. He isn't a genuine person, and I sensed he wasn't playing things straight."[225]

Michael filed extortion charges in late August against Evan Chandler and Barry Rothman. Rothman's legal secretary Geraldine Hughes overheard Chandler saying in response to the extortion charges, "It's my ass that's on the line and in danger of going to prison." The police opened an official extortion investigation; however, they never searched the homes and offices of Chandler and Rothman, nor did they convene a grand jury after the two refused to be interviewed.[226]

As a result of the extortion charges, Rothman removed himself from serving as Chandler's attorney. Chandler then hired civil attorney Larry Feldman in mid-September. Feldman then filed a $30 million civil lawsuit against Michael.[227] The lawsuit accused Michael of sexual battery, seduction, willful misconduct, emotional distress, fraud, and negligence.[228]

The filing of the civil suit created a situation where Michael had two pending cases against him simultaneously for the same matter, one criminal and one civil. Although the two cases were for the same alleged crime, one had nothing to do with the other. The police were investigating the criminal case, and the civil case was solely for the pursuit of compensation. In a criminal case, a defendant's freedom is on the line. If found guilty, the defendant may be imprisoned. In a civil case, only the defendant's bank balance is on the line. One cannot be incarcerated for losing a civil suit. A criminal case has a much higher burden of proof, requiring evidence "beyond a reasonable doubt" for conviction. In a civil lawsuit, the burden of proof is much lower, requiring only a "preponderance of evidence." To receive compensation, the plaintiff need only show that the accused was more likely than not to have committed the alleged acts. It is not uncommon for a given matter to be addressed in both a criminal and a civil court. However, it is highly unusual for an alleged criminal act to be tried in both simultaneously. Typically, criminal matters are first resolved in a criminal court, and after a conviction, the accuser may file a lawsuit.

On September 15, Michael was in Moscow, Russia, to perform a concert. The allegations were taking a toll on him. Michael's musical director, Brad Buxer, recounted how the two created the song "Stranger in Moscow" that morning. He stated, "Michael's going through a lot, as you can imagine. ... So, he calls me at 10:30 in the morning to come to his hotel. I come there, and he's really, really sad, and there's a piano there, and he goes, 'Just start playing something.' ... and he wrote beautiful lyrics to it ... and the song came together in that hour and a half that morning."[229] In the lyrics, Michael conveyed his isolation and desire to escape from fame and its resultant pressures.

The police went as hard as they could against Michael Jackson. They questioned close to thirty children and their families and approximately two hundred witnesses in total. They traveled to the Philippines and Australia on taxpayer money, searching for information. Several parents complained to Michael's attorney Bert Fields that the police officers told them unequivocally that Michael had molested their children despite their children denying it. The police falsely told the children that they had nude photos of them, trying to scare them into making allegations.[230]

Actor Corey Feldman, who had been sexually abused as a young actor in Hollywood, was one of the individuals interviewed. He was twenty-two at the time of the police interview.[231] In 2017, he recounted how the police had treated him. Feldman stated that he had tried to tell them that he had been abused, but not by Michael, but "All they cared about was trying to find something on Michael Jackson. ... I told them he is not that guy. And they said, 'Well, maybe you just don't understand your friend,' and I said, 'No, I know the difference between pedophiles and somebody who's not a pedophile because I've been molested. Here's the names. Go investigate.'" He said the police never investigated the names he gave them.[232]

Despite all the interviews, the police did not find a single credible corroborating witness against Michael, nor did they find any physical evidence to support the claims.

In early November, Michael's lawyers responded to the civil suit and requested that the lawsuit not go forward until the criminal case was closed. This is crucially important as the perception among much of the public is that Michael did not go to prison because he bought his way out of it. In reality, nothing could be further from the truth. It is Michael's attorneys who pushed for any criminal case to go first and Chandler's attorneys who pressed for the civil case to go first. So, the argument that Michael bought his way out of prison is patently false. Why would Jackson's lawyers want the criminal case to go first? In a criminal case, the defendant's life is on the line. He has the right to present his defense for the first time in a criminal courtroom. If he is forced to give away his defense in a civil deposition, then prosecutors can simply work around his defense in their criminal case. A deposition is testimony under oath in preparation for a civil trial. For example, if he shows that he has an alibi for a given set of dates, the prosecution can then simply change the dates when they file the criminal charges. As will be seen later, this is precisely what happened in the 2003 allegations against Michael. After learning of an alibi, the police simply changed the dates on their charge sheet.

Journalist John Ziegler explained:

> In these kinds of cases, dates and places are everything, and as soon as [Michael] gives where he was on any particular date or whether he was at a particular place or whatever, now the prosecution can craft their case around what he has already said under oath. ... Most of these cases ... are reverse-engineered, and to reverse-engineer a story, you need Michael Jackson on the record. Once you got him under oath, you can do whatever you want.[233]

Giving civil testimony prior to criminal testimony is the equivalent of giving the prosecution a front-row seat to your defense and allowing them to tailor their case around it. One of Michael's attorneys, Bonnie Eskenazi, expressed, "The prosecution should not be allowed to ride the coattails of civil discovery."[234]

The judge denied the request of Jackson's lawyers.[235] Michael's attorneys made multiple attempts to delay the civil case but were unsuccessful. Geraldine Hughes stated:

> It was obvious from a legal standpoint of view that the scales of justice were not pointing in Michael Jackson's favor. Instead, it was weighing heavily in favor of the thirteen-year-old boy [Jordan Chandler]. Michael Jackson's attorneys were applying precedent laws, which were applied in a similar sexual battery case. Pacers Inc. v. Superior Court specifically held that it is an improper invasion of the defendant's constitutional rights not to stay civil proceedings where a criminal investigation is ongoing. But Mr. Feldman's trump card was, "a child's memory is developing," and their inability to "remember like an adult."

Using this argument, Feldman filed a motion for Trial Preference for the civil proceedings, asking the trial to be held within 120 days. First, this request for an expedited civil trial hurt Jackson by taking away his right to present his defense for the first time in a criminal courtroom. Second, because the police had seized many of Jackson's personal records without providing him a copy of what they had taken in their police raids, he was limited in what he could gather for a defense in that shortened period of time.[236] The civil trial was set for March 21, 1994.[237] The judge ordered that Michael Jackson be deposed by January 1994.[238]

All of this was taking its toll on Michael. To add to his problems, he was recovering from surgery on his scalp to repair some of the damage from the burns. He was in tremendous physical pain. Friend David Nordahl shared:

> [Michael] was just going crazy. ... He let me feel it. They'd put a balloon under his skin on his scalp, and then they kept blowing that up. And he let me feel that huge thing sticking up in his head. And it was so painful. ... I told him ... "The best thing you can do is try to get something from the doctor to help you" because he was really in agony. And this was going on for a long period of time. So apparently, he had finally gotten something, and so he got hooked on it. ... I'm sure not understanding how easy it was to get addicted to some of the painkillers.[239]

Debbie Rowe, a medical assistant to Michael's dermatologist, Dr. Arnold Klein, revealed, "Michael had a huge amount of scarring on the top of his head, on the crown. ... He developed keloids. Keloids are extremely painful, thickening scars. ... Going in every week and having this balloon injected was extremely painful. ... His sensitivity to pain was just off the charts at this point. ... He was so afraid of the pain because the pain was so great."[240] Michael struggled on and off with painkillers for the rest of his life. Rowe explained that the pain from the scalp surgery was so great that it created within Michael such a fear of pain that even for minor procedures that, in the past, he had not had problems with, he would want painkillers.[241]

Michael's physical and emotional anguish came to a head in Mexico City in mid-November. His musical director, Brad Buxer, shared:

> We're in Mexico City doing eight shows in a row. … The first third of the show, we do a few songs, and then he goes off, and there's a break, and I'm playing the keyboards, and he's getting his makeup done or whatever, getting ready for the next part of the night and he's back there … and he's crying. He's sobbing. And he's sobbing because he doesn't know what the audience is thinking. He's terrified, and he comes out, and we get on with the night, but basically, the very last show we did in Mexico City … was probably the worst show I've ever seen him do. He still managed to pull it off, but he was sluggish, and he wasn't clear. Whatever was going on, it wasn't the normal Michael. … It was weird, but I knew how much pain he was going through, and he couldn't keep going on, so it was time for a break.[242]

Elizabeth Taylor intervened and checked Michael into a clinic to recover from his painkiller addiction. The rest of the tour was canceled. Michael's hairstylist, Carol LaMere, stated that she felt the painkiller addiction may have been as much from emotional pain as physical pain. She shared, "I think he was so sad that somebody would say that. He was so innocent with stuff; he couldn't understand that."[243] Buxer stated, however, that Michael did not stay away from music for long:

> Michael always worked and even in the worst points of Michael's life—and there were much worse points than then, with the first crazy crap that was going on with the horrible things that people said about him—he was always able to work. He's the strongest human being I've ever seen in my life. … When he got done with whatever he was doing, we got back to work.[244]

As the attorneys went back and forth regarding the scheduling of the civil trial, Michael was dealing with pain from the allegations, the salacious press coverage and innuendo, and his scalp burns. Meanwhile, the police, lacking evidence from their search of Michael's property and their interviews with witnesses, issued a warrant for a full body search of Michael. On December 20, they subjected him to a humiliating strip search.[245] The police photographed and took video of his genitalia and buttocks. Michael stated of the experience:

> I have been forced to submit to a dehumanizing and humiliating examination by the Santa Barbara County Sheriff's Department and the Los Angeles Police Department. ... The warrant stated that I had no right to refuse the examination ... and if I failed to cooperate with them, they would introduce that refusal at any trial as an indication of my guilt. It was the most humiliating ordeal of my life, one that no person should ever have to suffer. ... It was a nightmare, a horrifying nightmare.[246]

Michael's head of security at Neverland, Violet Gaitan, was on the property at the time of the body search. She stated, "I felt it was so personal, what they were doing to him ... just how they were going about it, it almost seemed like they just took pleasure in it. It was not a good day."[247]

Why did the police order a body search of Michael Jackson? They wanted to determine if Jordan's description of Michael's private parts was accurate. Why would Evan have Jordan offer a description if Michael had not molested him? According to Evan's brother Ray Chandler, Evan's attorney Larry Feldman had informed Evan that because of Michael's vitiligo, which constantly changes, "Anything Jordy says is irrelevant. It can change very quickly with this disease." Feldman expounded, "If he's right, he's right. And if he's wrong, we've got an explanation! ... It's a no-loser for us."[248] So, essentially, they figured it was harmless to guess where the blotches on Michael's skin were since even if they guessed wrong, it would not hurt their allegation.

So, did the description given by Jordan match the photographs by the police? No. Feldman made a bad miscalculation. He assumed the description would be determined to be right or wrong simply based on the location of the blotches. However, Jordan told the police that Michael was circumcised. Michael's autopsy report revealed that he was not circumcised.[249]

There were further indications that there was no match. For starters, the police did not detain Michael after the search. If they had determined a match, they likely would have arrested him. Then, in early January 1994, Evan's attorney, Larry Feldman, filed a motion in the civil case that contained a "multiple choice request." The options given were for Jackson to provide a copy of the police photographs or submit to a second body search, or for the court to bar the pictures from the civil trial as evidence.[250] Why would Feldman want to block the photographs from being introduced at the civil trial if Jordan had accurately described Michael's genitalia? The three options were all awful for Michael. Under the first, he would have to share intrusive photographs of his private parts with Feldman and his team. Under the second, he would have to submit to another humiliating body search. And under the third, the court would prohibit the photographs from being introduced as evidence of his innocence.

Another indication that the description did not match is the fact that Michael's mother, Katherine Jackson, was asked at a grand jury hearing in the spring of 1994 if her son had ever had surgery to alter his genitalia.[251] There would be no need to ask this question if the description matched.

Michael Jackson was originally scheduled to be deposed in the civil case on January 18, 1994, but on January 14, that deposition was moved to January 25.[252] His lawyers had been trying for months to get the judge to delay the civil proceedings until the criminal proceedings were complete, but to no avail. As a result, his attorneys settled the civil case on January 25, 1994, the day of Michael's scheduled deposition. At this same time, the extortion charges were dropped.[253]

The settlement amount was not disclosed, but the media have reported it to be in the $15–20 million range. According to *Court TV*, they were able to access a copy of the settlement, and $15,331,250 was paid to the accuser, as well as $1.5 million to each of his parents and $5 million to their attorney.[254] It is not clear who paid the settlement. In a motion at Michael's later 2005 trial, one of his attorneys, Brian Oxman, indicated that Michael's insurance company made the payment against Michael's wishes.[255] Indeed, Jordan Harriman, attorney for Transamerica Insurance Group, stated the company did make an offer to Jackson to resolve the claim, but it is not clear if that offer was accepted.[256] According to legal secretary Geraldine Hughes, at first the insurance company did not want to pay but they ultimately agreed to make the payment.[257] There may be a clue in Michael's music. In his 1995 song "Money," he sang, "Insurance, where do your loyalties lie?" According to the memorandum submitted by Oxman:

> It is general practice for an insurer to be entitled to control settlement negotiations, and the insured is precluded from any interference. ... Under the majority of contracts for liability insurance, the absolute control of the defense matter is turned over to the insurance company, and the insured is excluded from any interference in any negotiation for settlement. ... An insurance carrier has the right to settle claims covered by insurance when it decides settlement is expedient, and the insured may not interfere with nor prevent such settlements.[258]

While the main reason for the settlement was to protect Michael's right to offer his defense for the first time in a criminal courtroom, some close to the case indicated the decision to settle was related to the lawyers' reputations. Pellicano declared, "Can you imagine what would happen to an attorney who lost the Michael Jackson case? There's no way for all three lawyers to come out winners unless they settle. The only person who lost is Michael Jackson."[259]

In later years, Michael stated, "I didn't want to do a long, drawn-out thing on TV like OJ. ... It wouldn't look right. I just said, look, get this over with; I want to go on with my life. This is ridiculous. I've had enough. Go."[260]

The settlement did not prevent the Chandlers from participating in a criminal case, nor did it admit to any guilt on Michael Jackson's part. All it did was resolve the civil issue. Indeed, bribing someone to not testify in a trial is a felony under California law. Receiving such a bribe is also a felony.

According to Pellicano, "Michael wanted to fight and go through a trial."[261] If Michael had simply wanted to pay off the family, he could have easily done so back in August before the allegations were made public. Instead, he endured a humiliating ordeal in the press and during his police strip search.

After the settlement, the criminal investigation continued. Two grand juries were convened between February and April 1994, one in Los Angeles and one in Santa Barbara. Both declined to indict Michael Jackson.[262] It is often said that it's so easy to get an indictment that a "grand jury will indict a ham sandwich." However, in this case, the evidence was so lacking that not one but *two* grand juries refused to indict Michael Jackson.

The 1993 allegations as presented in the media do not match, in any way, shape, or form, the actual allegations. The reality is that a greedy and absent father deliberately went after Michael, seeking monetary compensation. He and his lawyers did everything they could to push the civil case ahead of the criminal case, while Michael's lawyers begged the judge to allow the criminal proceedings to go first. This was not a payment to silence a victim, as is often portrayed, but rather an elaborate extortion scheme. Indeed, Evan sued Michael again on May 7, 1996, this time asking for $60 million. In his suit, he claimed that Michael had breached the non-disclosure part of the settlement with the lyrics in his music. He also asked the court for permission to break the non-confidentiality agreement so that he could record his own album about the alleged molestation of his son. After approximately four years, the courts tossed out the case.[263]

And what of the boy at the center of it all, Jordan Chandler? How did all of this impact him? From his father's taped phone call, we know that the impact on the boy was "irrelevant" to his father. We also know a little bit about Jordan's possible thoughts based on the testimony of others. Michael's hairstylist, Carol LaMere, stated that Jordan had called Michael, crying, soon after the allegations hit the press. She said that Jordan was saying to Michael, "Why is my dad doing this?"[264]

In 1995, at age fourteen, Jordan legally emancipated himself from both of his parents.[265] June testified in 2005 that she had not spoken to her son in eleven years.[266] In Michael's 2005 trial, the prosecutors attempted to get Jordan to testify. According to an FBI file, Jordan told authorities he "had no interest in testifying against Jackson" and that he "would legally fight any attempt to do so."[267] Had Jordan testified, Michael Jackson's lawyer Tom Mesereau planned to call witnesses to testify that Jordan had privately confided in them that Michael had never molested him and that he would never talk to his parents again for what they made him say.[268] One such witness, Josephine Zohny, was interviewed in 2019 for the *Square One* documentary, a ground-breaking film detailing the 1993 allegations. In her interview, she stated of Jordan, "He said that he felt very used by his parents and that he wasn't close to them." She recounted the first time she heard him defend Michael. It was 2003, and the two were attending the same college program. Most in the program did not know that Jordan was the 1993 accuser. She said there was a discussion about whether or not Michael Jackson was a child molester:

> People were calling him a freak. These were people who did not have any fondness for Michael Jackson, and I chimed in with my belief that I didn't believe that Michael Jackson was a child molester. ... During that conversation, Jordan Chandler chimed in and said that he, too, thought Michael Jackson wasn't capable of the things he was being accused of, and he said that voluntarily

and he said it without my prompting, and he wasn't asked. He wasn't in the direct conversation; I was arguing with a group of maybe three other people. He was seated close to us, but he wasn't in on this discussion, and throughout the semester, there were different occasions like that where he would reaffirm things that I said in defense of Michael Jackson. ... It really affirmed my belief that Michael was innocent, and given things that Jordan had said separately ... about his home life, it affirmed my belief that he was a victim of his parents' greed and that he was forced to say certain things because I really have a hard time believing that if he had been molested by Michael Jackson, he would be going out of his way to say he didn't think he was capable of these things.[269]

On August 5, 2005, less than two months after Michael's acquittal in his 2005 child molestation trial, Jordan obtained a temporary restraining order against his father, claiming his father "struck him on the head from behind with a twelve and one-half pound weight and then sprayed his eyes with mace or pepper spray and tried to choke him."[270] Did Evan's physical attack on his son have anything to do with Michael's acquittal and Jordan's refusal to testify against Michael?

Evan Chandler died of a gunshot wound to the head on November 5, 2009, a few months after Michael's death. The police ruled Evan's death a suicide. Evan was allegedly suffering from a debilitating illness at the time of his death.[271]

The law in California ultimately changed to allow prosecutors to intervene in a civil action and halt it until a criminal case is complete. According to District Attorney Tom Sneddon, who was the DA who went after Michael in both 1993 and again in the 2000s, it was the Michael Jackson case that led to the changing of the law.[272]

Raymond Chandler, Evan's brother, wrote in his 2004 book concerning the allegations, "Had Michael paid the twenty million dollars demanded of him in August, rather than the following January, he might have spent the next ten years as the world's most famous entertainer, instead of the world's most infamous child molester."[273]

It is evident from the timeline of events that the settlement was purely to protect Michael's right to present his defense for the first time in a criminal courtroom. It was not, as often claimed, a payoff to escape prison time. Indeed, it was the Chandlers who tried to rush the civil case to precede the criminal and Michael's lawyers who pushed for the criminal case to happen first. Had Michael wanted to pay his way out of his troubles, he could have given Evan the screenwriting deal he'd sought in the summer of 1993. Instead, he allowed the allegations to go public, suffered through a humiliating ordeal, had his home and his condo searched, had many of his friends, staff, and acquaintances questioned, and subjected himself to a mortifying and invasive body search, which he was legally not obliged to agree to but did so as any refusal could have been used against him in a criminal trial. This was all happening as he was trying to recover from painful surgery to repair the third-degree burns on his scalp, creating a dependency on painkillers, no doubt aggravated by emotional stress. Physical pain can be much more harrowing when one is also under psychological strain.

To add to all of this, the media printed one salacious, unsubstantiated story after another. Michael expressed his anger at the press, "At every opportunity, the media has dissected and manipulated these allegations to reach their own conclusions."[274]

As for Evan Chandler, the reader must ask themselves, what parent would push for a civil payout and then distance themselves from the criminal case if they were genuinely concerned that the accused was a child molester? What kind of parent could enjoy the luxury of millions of dollars knowing that the accused was walking freely and continuing to molest other children? Would not the material wealth be a constant reminder that others are suffering?

The allegations against Michael Jackson in 1993 do not even remotely meet the most minimal burden of proof. But they ruined Michael's life and his reputation. Michael responded to the ordeal the only way he knew how—through his music.

9

The Response

It's the most anti-establishment album you will ever hear by a mainstream pop star. - Investigative journalist Charles Thomson

Michael's frustration, pain, and anger over the accusations boiled over into his next album, *HIStory*, released on June 20, 1995. Michael capitalized the first three letters of the title to convey that history depends on who tells it, and he was going to use the album to tell his story. Investigative journalist Charles Thomson described the album: "It's anti-police, it's anti-military, it's anti-banker, it's anti-corporate, it's anti-lawyer, anti-insurance. He's ripping the shits out of everyone. … It's just furious." Many consider *HIStory* to be Michael's magnum opus. He did not hold back.

The album launched with much controversy. For the opening teaser video, the press accused Michael of copying Hitler's *Triumph of the Will*, which he denied. When asked if he'd watched the Hitler film, Michael replied, "I watch everything."[275]

The first song he released off the album was a duet with his sister Janet, titled "Scream." In the lyrics, he raged against the media's lies and condemned their "schemes" and "collusions," proclaiming that the entire system of power was awful and crooked. He spoke of how the media corrupted many, but he desired to maintain his soul and not sell out. He also declared that the press was controlling the narrative, causing people to be confused about what is really true.

From the very first song, the listener can feel Michael's anger. It is palpable. The second song on the album, also released as a single, was "They Don't Care About Us." The lyrics were highly controversial. As with all songs, its meaning is open to interpretation. It began by describing our divisive and often thoughtless society. Michael then questioned the use of violence as a solution to problems. In the accompanying music video, he displayed an image of Lee Harvey Oswald, President John F. Kennedy's alleged assassin, being shot by gangster Jack Ruby in the background as Michael lamented over the violence.

Michael then conveyed his strength to resist the attacks on him. After that came the most controversial lyrics in the song: "Jew me, sue me." After the album's initial release, some of these lyrics were censored, and a loud sound was placed over the original words. In Evan Chandler's 1996 lawsuit against Michael, Evan claimed that Michael was referring to him with these lyrics since Evan was Jewish and had sued Michael for child molestation.[276] The media labeled the song as anti-Semitic. Michael, however, did not have a hateful bone in his body. He was expressing how those in power use divide-and-conquer tactics as a weapon. In the same verse, he proclaimed, "Don't you black or white me." He then sang about what might be interpreted as his feelings about the sexual molestation allegations leveled at him, which he then extrapolated to the pain and suffering of all who have been attacked and abused. He revealed that he was tired of being the victim of "hate" and "shame" and proclaimed that his pride was being "raped" as his image was being destroyed.

Michael released two videos to accompany the song. He filmed one of them in a poor region of Brazil and the other, more controversial one, in a prison. In the second, he is locked and chained in a cell, with many TVs in the cell's walls with what appears to be an all-seeing eye surrounding each of them. The prison cell looks like an Orwellian nightmare, conveying that we all live in confinement and are being watched and subjugated to some extent. Throughout the video, many atrocities from human history are displayed. The music video TV channels rarely played the video due to its graphic and controversial nature.

In the song "This Time Around," Michael proclaimed that he could not be controlled. In the song "D.S.," he sang about District Attorney Tom Sneddon, the man coming after him for the child molestation allegations. The official lyrics list the name as Dom Sheldon, likely to avoid a lawsuit, but they sound similar to Tom Sneddon phonetically. In the lyrics, Michael questioned if the CIA was involved in the attempts to destroy him.

He also referenced the CIA in another song on the album, "Tabloid Junkie." This song is about media manipulation and covers the JFK assassination. Michael sang about the use of slander as a powerful weapon, then wrote of how the press "mutilated" JFK's image after his murder. Instead of portraying him as the thoughtful and conscientious man he was, they "resurrected" him as a dopey playboy. Michael then declared that the truth lay at the "grassy knoll" and he made it clear that multiple shooters gunned down JFK because of the threat he posed to those in power. The grassy knoll is the location from where many believe a second shooter was stationed in the JFK assassination.

Though it is not clear if Michael is still referring to the Kennedy assassination in the second verse, the lyrics nonetheless are applicable. He sings about shooting with the intent to kill, then afterward blaming the victim for his own death while shedding fake tears of sympathy. Those who have studied the Kennedy assassination know that the press blamed JFK for the lax security along his motorcade route. In other words, they essentially blamed him for his own death. After Kennedy's murder, the establishment greatly sympathized, but were the tears fake, as Michael implied?

In the second verse, Michael also referred to the press's lies about his vitiligo and how they were shaming the race. In the song's chorus, Michael implored listeners not to trust the media blindly and not to fall so easily for propaganda.

In the song "Money," Michael sang about how greed runs the world. In the opening verse, he questioned whether the wars we fight are for the reasons we claim or whether they are fought for selfish reasons. In the second verse, he discussed the lengths to which people will go to secure profits.

In the song "HIStory," Michael asked how long we'll keep repeating the same mistakes, i.e., for how long must people endure agony, fight wars, and bomb children before we put an end to the senseless suffering.

In "Earth Song," Michael shared his love and concern for nature and humanity. At the song's end, he questioned how the world became the way it is. How did we reach a point where the environment is collapsing? Why is the Holy Land torn apart? Why is the common man still not free? And why are we ignoring the pain of so many?

"Earth Song" meant a lot to Michael. Big Al recounted the moment he first learned of the song from Michael prior to its release:

> I hadn't seen him in several months, ... he gave me a really big hug. ... Then he starts talking about he's been in New York and he's working on the *HIStory* album which hadn't been released yet ... [and] he starts talking about "Earth Song" and he just went on and on and on ... about "Earth Song." ... You can hear in his voice and see in his eyes how passionate he was about it, and I felt like an idiot because I had no idea what he was talking about and he's talking to me like I was in the studio with him for the last eight months. ... When the conversation was all over, the first thing I'm thinking is I really can't wait to hear that song. ... He was just so excited about telling me about that song. He just went on and on

and on.[277] … He almost started crying. He was so passionate about this song.[278]

HIStory was Michael's most personal album. His anger and hurt are evident throughout. It took tremendous courage for him to write and sing the songs he did. They certainly were not typical pop songs. And with it he undoubtedly put an even bigger target on his back than he already had.

10

The Quiet Years

We were watching a movie. There was a scene where they talked poorly about my uncle. I just remember it hurting him, and I remember him getting up and leaving.
– Taryll Jackson

From the late 1990s to the early 2000s, the world of Michael Jackson was relatively quiet. He was still making music but was less hands-on than in earlier years. He toured globally to promote the *HIStory* album, starting in September 1996, and finishing in October 1997. The tour only hit one US city: Honolulu, Hawaii. Big Al attended the Hawaii concerts and told Michael afterward, "I saw the show last night ... I had no idea that you worked so hard to keep us all employed ... and he laughed. He appreciated it." Neverland, on average, employed approximately one hundred staff at any given time, mostly grounds crew.[279]

Michael released a remix album on May 20, 1997, *Blood on the Dance Floor*. Though the record consisted mainly of remixes, it did include five new songs. The album received little promotion in the U.S. but still managed to become the greatest-selling remix album of all time. Two songs worth noting on the album are "Morphine" and "Is It Scary." In "Morphine," Michael sang about his struggles with painkillers and how, despite his distrust, the drugs were seducing him.

In "Is It Scary," Michael reflected on how society viewed him as a freak, but questioned whether that label belongs not to the one who is judged but the one who judges. He asked: Would a mirror reveal the truth? He reflected on the fear displayed by some towards his eccentricities and proclaimed that he was just as scared of those who feared him as they were of him.

In 1998, Michael wrote the song "People of the World" to raise money for schools impacted by the Great Hanshin earthquake in Japan. As with many of his previous songs, he urged all peoples and all countries to come together and sing in harmony.

Michael followed up the *Blood on the Dance Floor* album with the *Invincible* album, released on October 30, 2001. *Invincible* also received little promotion. Nonetheless, it still became one of the twenty top-selling albums of the decade. Michael felt Sony was unwilling to put great effort into promoting the album because they wanted to weaken him financially and force him to sell his 50 percent stake in the Sony/ATV music catalog. Sony, on the other hand, knew that Michael had no desire to renew his contract with them and may have felt no need to put significant money and effort into promoting an artist who was planning to leave the label.[280]

Invincible was arguably weaker than Michael's previous work. This was largely because Michael only wrote two of the songs, in contrast to his prior albums, where he had written much of the music. He wrote many, though not all, of his iconic hits.[281] It is not fully clear why he was so much more hands-off with the album, but it likely was related to his having children and wanting to put more time and effort into raising them. When he did record, he brought his children into the studio. His son, Prince, often ran around while his father was recording. Studio engineer CJ de Villar shared, "There were three sessions where I actually ended up holding Prince while Michael was recording his vocals. I would be at the console, working with one arm and Prince in the other."[282]

Perhaps another reason Michael was more hands-off is because he did not have as much to say as he had in the past and was merely fulfilling a contractual obligation. For the prior album, *HIStory*, Michael was reeling from the child molestation allegations and had a lot to get off his chest. Nonetheless, Michael did write some great music in the latter years of his life, but for whatever reason, he never released it. Many promising songs were recorded for *Invincible* that were never placed on the album, such as the powerful anti-war anthem Michael co-wrote, "We've Had Enough." In the song, he questioned the morality of war and whether anyone other than God has the right to decide who gets to live and who must die. The song was ultimately included in a 2004 CD box set.

For *Invincible*, Michael chose a much tamer set of songs to ultimately place on the album, ones that were primarily created by others. Nevertheless, his creativity remained strong. Close collaborator Brad Buxer said, "The very, most beautiful stuff that we ever did, ever, was at the end. It just kept getting better and better." Many of these songs never saw the light of day. Two of the tunes given as samples by Buxer were "Days of Gloucestershire" and "I Am a Loser." Rough versions of both have been leaked on the internet.[283]

In June of 1999, Michael suffered another horrible accident while perform-ing. A bridge he was standing on collapsed. He suffered a severe back injury and, as a result, once again struggled with painkillers.[284] Michael always loved music. Still, he wanted to explore other artistic areas that would not require him to give grueling performances. He said about touring, "I love to entertain, but I don't like the system of touring. You're jet lagged. You're sleepy on stage. I don't know where I am half the time. ... Then you get to your hotel, and your adrenaline is at its zenith, and you can't fall asleep, and you've got a show the next day. It's tough."[285]

Michael was particularly interested in directing films. He had always put a lot of effort into his music videos, which he called short films. In 1999, Michael attempted to buy Marvel for $1.4 billion, but the deal ultimately fell through. Marvel owned the rights to many comic book characters, including Spider-Man, the Hulk, Iron Man, and the X-Men. According to Michael's business advisor at the time, Dieter Wiesner, "Marvel was the plan for the second half of Michael's life. He had the Beatles catalog on one side, and if he bought the Marvel catalog, he had the second part." In 2009, Disney bought Marvel for $4 billion, and Marvel-character film franchises have brought in billions in revenue. "Michael was right; he knew what was coming," said Wiesner.[286]

On March 6, 2001, Michael spoke at Oxford University about children's issues. Despite the allegations, he did not shy away from talking about an issue so dear to his heart:

> Childhood has become the great casualty of modern-day living. … Today's children are constantly encouraged to grow up faster as if the period known as childhood is a burdensome stage to be endured and ushered through as swiftly as possible. And on that subject, I am certainly one of the world's greatest experts. Ours is a generation that has witnessed the abrogation of the parent-child covenant. … This violation has bred a new generation. Generation O, let us call it. … The O stands for a generation that has everything on the outside—wealth, success, fancy clothing, and fancy cars, but an aching emptiness on the inside.[287]

Despite the limited promotion, Michael did perform two concerts to promote the *Invincible* album. They were both in New York City, one on September 7, 2001, and the other on September 10, 2001, the night before the September 11 attacks. According to Michael's brother Jermaine, Michael had a meeting at the World Trade Center on the morning of September 11, but he overslept and did not attend.[288] Michael wrote a song, "What More Can I Give," to raise funds for the victims of 9/11. Many artists participated in singing the song, a la "We Are the World." Sony, however, did not release the tune as a single, which further fractured Michael's relationship with them.

With respect to his personal life, Michael briefly married Lisa Marie Presley, from 1994 until 1996. Though the marriage was short, the relationship lasted approximately eight years. They became friends in 1992, and the two continued to spend time together for four years after the divorce.[289] According to studio engineer Rob Hoffman, "They acted like two kids in love. They held hands all the time, and she hung out at the studio for quite a while. I never questioned their love for one another."[290] Lisa Marie told friends that Michael was "the kindest person she had ever met."[291]

In the late 1990s, Michael had two children with Debbie Rowe. She was a medical assistant whom he had known since the early 1980s. She had helped treat him for his various ailments: lupus, vitiligo, and the burns on his scalp. It appears that Rowe was essentially a surrogate. She gave full custody of the children to Michael. He had a third child in 2002, also believed to be born via a surrogate. One of the reasons given for his divorce from Presley is that Michael very much wanted to have children. Presley was unsure about having children with Michael due to the extraordinary fame and resultant pressures surrounding him. She was uncertain about bringing children into such an environment.[292]

Those who knew Michael all said he was a fabulous father who worked hard to ensure his children did not become spoiled. Friend David Nordahl shared a story of attending the seventh birthday of Michael's oldest child, Prince, "I was anxious to see what kind of presents he got. I was so shocked because he didn't get anything that was over $2. All of the things that he got for his birthday were things that I consider to be stocking stuffers. ... And he was absolutely thrilled to get them. Things like Play-Doh." Many think Michael named his son Prince because everyone called Michael the "King of Pop." But that is inaccurate. His grandfather's name, on his mother's side, was Prince Scruse. Michael adored his grandfather and named his son after him.[293]

The kids were not allowed to play video games or watch videos unless they earned points through their schoolwork.[294] Michael's daughter Paris told an interviewer that she and her brothers had to read books for currency in her father's house. If they wanted a toy, they had to read books to earn it. And he would quiz them on what they read.[295] Every morning, the kids had to clean up their rooms and make their beds before coming down for breakfast.[296] Paris said, "My dad was really good about making sure we were cultured, making sure we were educated, and not just showing us the glitz and glam, like hotel hopping five-star places, but ... we saw everything, we saw third-world countries, we saw every part of the spectrum."[297] Prince said his dad was very spiritual, "He used to talk about how beautiful the world is and who could have made something so beautiful. ... We used to talk about God a lot. He used to just marvel at everything. ... He was very emotional."[298] In another interview, Prince stated:

> Some of my earliest memories with my dad really involved going to children's hospitals and less fortunate neighborhoods. He always wanted us to be aware that even though we live a certain lifestyle ... that is not how the majority of the world lives. So, he really wanted to expose us to how the other side lives so that we can have appreciation and gratitude for what we have but also so that we could understand the importance of giving back. Because you're only here for a certain amount of time, and what matters is how you interact with people here.[299]

Michael continued to be impacted by the abuse allegations during this period of his life, which might partly explain why he stepped back from the limelight to some extent. He was the butt of many jokes during these years, and the media was especially harsh towards him. His nephew Taryll Jackson recounted how quickly his uncle could go from upbeat to sad:

> We were watching a movie. There was a scene where they talked poorly about my uncle. I just remember it hurting him, and I

remember him getting up and leaving. It was really sad, and it really hurt and upset him. We didn't finish the movie. We stopped, and we all went out to see him, and he said, trying to be strong, "You guys go watch the rest of the movie; I'm OK," and we said we don't even care to see it. ... It just showed me the pain. He's human. ... It really bothered me that he had to go through that, and I hate ... that I had to see that.[300]

The jokes were endless. Rapper Eminem released a video making fun of Michael allegedly liking boys and making fun of the burns on his scalp. When Michael was asked about the Eminem video mocking him, he replied, "To have him do something like that was pretty painful. ... He should be ashamed of himself. ... I've been an artist most of my life, and I've never attacked another fellow artist. Great artists don't do that."[301]

As harsh as the jokes could be, they would only get worse.

11

Not Again

[Michael] came up and he rolls his window down and he is crying. I'm seeing tears coming from his eyes. ... In my head I'm going what was in this documentary. ... We were literally trying to comfort Michael Jackson. - Fan Jenny Winings

By the early 2000s, Michael Jackson's image was a mess. Countless jokes were being made about him. Many viewed him as a strange and odd character who had perhaps molested a child. Most of what the public understood about Michael came from a slanted press. Michael, however, did not help himself with what was perhaps excessive plastic surgery and an on-and-off drug dependency born from genuine physical ailments due to injuries to his scalp and back, likely exacerbated by the emotional strain of the press attacks. There is no doubt that Michael Jackson was bullied publicly, and severely so.

To repair his image, Michael decided to participate in a documentary. He hoped to clarify the many distortions in his public persona and convey his true self. Unfortunately, this effort backfired to a colossal extent and caused Michael irreparable damage. Martin Bashir was a British filmmaker who had recently interviewed Princess Diana. Michael greatly admired the princess and felt Bashir did a great job with her, so he believed Bashir could do the same for him and agreed to do extensive interviews with him.

Bashir, however, had his own agenda. What ultimately aired was a highly manipulative hit piece that insinuated Michael was a disturbed man with a sick and worrisome obsession with children. The documentary first aired in the UK on February 3, 2003. Michael Jackson fan Jenny Winings was waiting outside Michael's hotel with another fan on the morning of February 4 in hopes of seeing the star. She recounted his distraught reaction:

> The documentary was airing in London on a Thursday night, and we were in America. We knew it was airing, but we didn't see it, obviously. Friday morning, the morning after it aired ... [Michael] came up, and he rolls his window down, and he is crying. I'm seeing tears coming from his eyes. And Joann [another fan] and I are in shock. ... And he said, "They're saying that I did these things again, and they're saying I do these terrible things to kids. ... I would never do that; I cannot believe this is happening again." And we're just standing there in shock. ... In my head, I'm going, "What was in this documentary?" ... We were literally trying to comfort Michael Jackson.[302]

In the documentary, Michael is seen with a young twelve-year-old boy, Gavin Arvizo, sitting next to him. Gavin has his head on Michael's shoulder and is holding his hand. It would come out later that Bashir had asked Michael to hold Gavin's hand.[303] Gavin had been diagnosed with a rare cancer, and his dream was to meet Michael Jackson. Michael's hairstylist, Carol LaMere, had met the Arvizo family through her son's dance class, and they begged her to arrange a meeting with Michael. She said she would normally not have agreed but gave in due to Gavin's cancer. She said she now regrets that decision every day of her life.[304] Michael invited the Arvizos to Neverland, and they visited on multiple occasions. For the most part, Michael was not on the property, but even when he was, he at times told the Arvizos he was not there. Later in court, Gavin testified how Michael claimed to not be on the property, but Gavin saw him and was upset that Michael was avoiding them.[305] For the documentary, Bashir asked Michael if they could film with some of the kids Michael had helped over the years, and Michael gave Bashir some options, including the Arvizos.

Gavin filmed for the documentary in September 2002, and during the shooting, he recalled his first visit to Neverland in the summer of 2000, "There was one night I asked him [Michael] if I could stay in his bedroom. He let me stay in the bedroom, and I was like, 'Michael, you can sleep on the bed,' and he was like, 'No, no, you sleep on the bed.' And he finally said, 'If you love me, you'll sleep on the bed.'" Michael slept on the floor with his assistant Frank Cascio, and Gavin and his brother slept in the bed.[306] Frank was not in the documentary, but he later stated that Michael had asked him to sleep in the room since he felt the kids were being pushy and might have ulterior motives but did not have the heart to tell them no.[307] Bashir then asked Michael if it was appropriate for a man to allow kids to sleep in his bed, to which Michael replied, "Why can't you share your bed? The most loving thing you can do is share your bed with someone. You can have my bed if you want, sleep in it. I'll sleep on the floor. ... Always give the best to the company."[308] The press chopped up the interview and repeatedly aired the snippets, "If you love me, you'll sleep on the bed," and "The most loving thing you can do is share your bed with someone." They left out that Michael and his assistant slept on the floor, that Gavin shared the bed with his brother, and that the two boys had asked to sleep in the room. The entire world started speculating 24/7 once again that Michael Jackson was a child molester. It can certainly be argued that Michael was naïve, gullible, easily manipulated, and overly generous, but it is clear from the unedited interview that molestation did not occur, and Michael did not even sleep in the bed with Gavin. Indeed, Gavin himself never claimed to have been molested on that night.

Michael's ex-wife, Lisa Marie Presley, gave her thoughts on what Michael said in the interview regarding sharing his bed:

I think he said that stuff sometimes to be defiant because he got so angry at having been accused. He was such a stubborn little rebel at times, and he was like a child, and he would just say what he felt everyone didn't want him to say. I don't feel like he had a straight head during those things, and I think that they were edited in a very, very manipulative, nasty way.[309]

As a result of the media firestorm, Michael had his team quickly put together a rebuttal documentary, sharing the unaired footage. While Bashir was taping his interviews, Michael's cameraman had also been secretly recording, unbeknownst to Bashir. The rebuttal documentary showed the many places where Bashir had taken comments out of context. During this time, the press was hounding the Arvizos, so the family reached out to actor Chris Tucker to see if they could stay with him until the press bombardment died down. Chris was on his way to Florida. The Arvizos informed him that Michael was also in Florida and asked him if he could drop them off where Michael was, and Chris agreed. The Arvizos then flew back to California with Michael around February 7 and 8, after which they stayed at Neverland briefly until the media hoopla calmed down. While at Neverland, they agreed to partake in the rebuttal documentary.[310] Their last day on the property was March 12.[311]

Gavin was thirteen then, and he and his family were very upbeat during the rebuttal recording and effusive in their praise of Michael. They recorded their segment on February 20, 2003.[312] However, things quickly turned sour. Michael's staff testified that the Arvizos began to act entitled and were rude to them.[313] Actor Chris Tucker warned Michael about the Arvizo family, informing him how they had tried to take advantage of him.[314] Michael's lawyer, Tom Mesereau, stated, "This family began to come up with these allegations ... only when they realized that they were on the way out, that Michael Jackson was sick of them, didn't want to deal with them anymore, didn't want them on his property."[315] Gavin himself testified in court that he felt Michael had abandoned him and his family.[316]

During this period that the Arvizos were on the Neverland property, both the Santa Barbara Sheriff's Department and the Santa Barbara Department of Children and Family Services (DCFS) began investigating the potential molestation of Gavin by Michael. The dean of Gavin's school also questioned him in the days after the documentary aired. Gavin denied to all that he was being molested.[317] However, eventually he changed his tune.

In February 2003, Gavin's mother, Janet Arvizo, contacted attorney William Dickerman allegedly to help her retrieve items from storage. However, Dickerman then brought on Larry Feldman. Feldman was the attorney who had won the large settlement for Evan Chandler in the 1993 molestation allegations against Michael. Feldman sent the Arvizos to Dr. Stanley Katz, a psychologist specializing in child sexual abuse. Because the laws in California had changed since the 1993 allegations, the Arvizos, who up to this point were dealing only with civil attorneys, were forced first to go the criminal route if they wanted a big payout. Only after completing the criminal case could they pursue their civil claims. Feldman, as such, phoned the Santa Barbara Sheriff's Department in June to inform them of the allegations, which the sheriff's department had already been investigating since February, when the documentary aired. From July through September 2003, investigators conducted several interviews with the Arvizos.[318]

On November 18, 2003, the police issued an arrest warrant for Michael Jackson and raided his Neverland ranch. Over seventy officers participated. Head of Safety and Human Resources at Neverland, Violet Gaitan, recounted:

> It was a complete shock. It felt like an assault because you can't stop it, and it was scary because they came in, they're armed. ... All of a sudden, all these cars are coming in, all these helicopters. ... It was very alarming; it was scary. ... There was more to it than them just doing their job. It felt very personal. ... They came with this idea of what they were going to find, and it just wasn't there.[319]

Michael was in Las Vegas at the time, shooting a music video, one of the last obligations he owed Sony before being free of his contract. Upon arriving in Santa Maria, he was handcuffed and taken into custody. Bail was set at $3 million, which he posted.[320] Michael said of the arrest, "They did it to try and belittle me, to take away my pride, but I went through the whole system with them." Michael also claimed that the police were abusive, tying the handcuffs too tightly behind his back, "They put it in a certain position, knowing it's going to hurt me, affect my back. Now I can't move. It keeps me from sleeping at night. I can't sleep." Michael also claimed the police mocked him:

> One time I asked to use the restroom, and they said, "Sure, it's right around the corner there." Once I went into the restroom, they locked me in there for like forty-five minutes. There was doo-doo, feces thrown all over the walls, the floor, the ceiling, and it stunk so bad. And one of the policemen came by the window, and he made a sarcastic remark. He said, "Does it smell good enough for you in there? How do you like the smell? Is it good?" And I just simply said, "It's alright." They did this on purpose.[321]

The sheriff's department filed a statement of probable cause on November 17. It claimed that the molestation occurred between the dates of February 7, 2003, and March 10, 2003.[322] These dates are crucial because the claim is that Michael began molesting Gavin *after* the Bashir documentary aired, i.e., he began molesting Gavin at the time that the entire world was already speculating that he was molesting him, as the police and DCFS were already investigating him for molesting Gavin. This claim, if true, would make Michael Jackson one of the dumbest criminals known to mankind. The Arvizos had to come up with such dates because it was clear from the unedited Bashir documentary taped in the fall of 2002 that Michael was not molesting Gavin, and Gavin did not see Michael again until after the documentary aired. In the statement of probable cause, Gavin claimed that he had been molested at least five times during the one-month period.

On December 18, 2003, the sheriff's department officially filed charges against Michael Jackson. The charges repeated the molestation dates as having occurred between February 7 and March 10. It claimed the molestation occurred seven times, five that Gavin remembered, and two that his brother saw while Gavin was asleep.[323]

However, as investigators prepared for the Jackson trial, they encountered several major obstacles. First, they came across a videotape that the Arvizos had taped for Michael Jackson's rebuttal documentary. The Arvizos were never included in the final version of the aired rebuttal documentary; nevertheless, a copy of their taped interview remained. The interview was recorded on February 20, 2003. The video included not just the official interview but also all the in-between chitchat. The Arvizos profusely praised Michael in the video, made fun of Bashir, and claimed that Bashir's insinuations about molestation were absurd.[324] So how did the police respond to this? They added a conspiracy charge to Michael's list of charges. They claimed that Michael had conspired with unindicted co-conspirators to kidnap and imprison the Arvizos to force them to participate in the rebuttal documentary. They claimed the video was scripted, even though it clearly showed chitchat between official filming. However, this did not solve the police's problems because they also discovered that Michael Jackson had an ironclad alibi for the early dates of the alleged molestation. Did the police drop the charges after uncovering proof that Gavin had lied to them about the dates of the alleged molestation? No. When the original timeline proved false, the police merely created an even more preposterous timeline. They moved the dates of the alleged molestation from a start date of February 7 to a new start date of February 20. Gavin testified in court that the molestation began sometime after the taping of the rebuttal documentary.[325]

So, essentially, now the allegation was that Michael kidnapped the family as the entire world was speculating that he was molesting Gavin and as the police and DCFS were investigating him for the same. Michael then allegedly forced the Arvizos to tape a video saying he was not molesting Gavin, and then after all that, Michael molested Gavin for the very first time. This is the timeline that the police went to court with. Investigative reporter Charles Thomson summed up the alleged events, "They have Michael Jackson abducting a family and holding them against their will so that he can force them to deny on videotape a series of acts of molestation which he's not yet committed. ... The whole case makes no sense whatsoever."[326] During a videotaped police interview, Gavin claimed that he and his family were scared while they were at Neverland for fear that Michael and his alleged co-conspirators "might kill us."[327] At trial Janet Arvizo claimed that she felt her children might be abducted from Neverland via a hot-air balloon.[328]

The timeline was not the only thing to change between the initial charges and the trial. Gavin initially claimed he was molested five times; then, in court, he changed his story to say he was only molested twice.[329] Perhaps this was due to the now shortened time frame in which the alleged molestation occurred. Under normal circumstances, if the police had an alleged victim who had initially given them the wrong dates and then drastically changed the number of times he claimed to have been molested, would they not consider dropping the case due to credibility issues? Apparently not if the accused is Michael Jackson.

The trial began on February 28, 2005. Musical collaborator Brad Buxer shared that he and Michael worked on music all the way up to the beginning of the trial. "[Michael was] stronger than anyone I have ever seen. ... We were still doing music up to that point. Me? I wouldn't be able to get out of bed," said Buxer. "I'd be paralyzed. ... He was still working on music. ... Obviously, he was scared. ... [But] the best stuff we ever did was at the end of 2004. ... There was less laughter, but musically, the most creative stuff we've ever done was being done."[330]

Reporter Aphrodite Jones recounted the moment she first saw Michael arrive at the courthouse:

As I'm standing there, the motorcade arrived. Everyone got out of their cars except for Michael. And he was in his car by himself. ... He was still sitting in the car. There's 2400 credentialed media all around him, and behind that are ... a thousand fans ... screaming. So, you have thousands of people with cameras and screaming, and he's about to get out of this car and walk into a courthouse for a criminal trial. And I'll never forget seeing his face because I was standing right there, and I could see it through the windshield, and he had the loneliest look I've ever seen on any human being in my life. He looked so alone, and so, I don't want to say afraid, but it was so surreal because here are all these people screaming, here are all these cameras clicking before he even got out of the car, and this person was just completely and totally alone.[331]

At trial, it was revealed that the Arvizos had a sordid history and a pattern of using others for financial gain. Gavin had reached out to and met many celebrities, including George Lopez, Chris Tucker, and Kobe Bryant.[332] After Gavin reached out to comedian and late-night talk show host Jay Leno, Leno described him as "scripted." Leno's assistant told him she would have the boy stop calling.[333] Multiple teachers of Gavin's had complained about his bad behavior. One called him "defiant" and "disrespectful" with "good acting skills."[334] Actor George Lopez testified that both Gavin and his father, David, constantly asked him for money. After Lopez found Gavin's wallet left behind at Lopez's home, Gavin's father accused Lopez of stealing a large sum of money from it. Lopez ultimately distanced himself from the family. He called David Arvizo an "extortionist" to his face. The Arvizos tried to hold multiple fundraisers for Gavin's cancer even though he had medical insurance.[335]

Michael Jackson was not the first person whom the Arvizos accused of sexual abuse. After security guards followed Gavin out of a JCPenny store for shoplifting, his mother accused the guards of sexually abusing her and was able to get a $152,000 settlement out of the store.[336] Janet then committed welfare fraud by not disclosing the settlement payments.[337]

As for the alleged imprisonment at Neverland, the Arvizos often left the property during their "captivity." Janet Arvizo regularly visited a local beauty salon on Michael's tab. Jury foreman Paul Rodriguez stated, "What she probably should have done is call the police. There's all these phones in the area. ... Instead, she gets her legs waxed."[338] The kids went to see dentists and to buy toys.[339] The Arvizos also claimed they were not allowed to know what time it was, but there are large clocks all over the Neverland property.[340]

To boost their feeble allegations, prosecutors may have attempted to manufacture evidence. During the police raid of Neverland, they found magazines depicting naked women in Michael Jackson's bedroom. Because the magazines implied Michael was a typical heterosexual male, they argued that Michael had shown these magazines to Gavin to prepare him for molestation. At the grand jury proceedings, District Attorney Tom Sneddon handed adult magazines found at Neverland to Gavin Arvizo and then sent them out for fingerprint analysis. Fabricating evidence is a felony. Michael's attorney asked Gavin's brother, Star, if one of the magazines introduced as evidence by the prosecutors was the magazine that Michael had shown him and his brother. The boy repeatedly replied that Michael had definitely shown them the magazine. Michael's attorney then pointed out to the court that the magazine was published almost a year after the Arvizos had last been to Neverland. The boy then quickly changed his story and said it was not the same magazine. But Sneddon had been caught red-handed. Jurors were seen rolling their eyes.[341]

Indeed, the Arvizos constantly contradicted themselves and each other as they testified. One of the female jurors stated of Janet Arvizo's testimony, "A lot of the parts of her testimony I wanted to just break out laughing, but I couldn't."[342] Another juror stated, "There was nothing ... that was able to convince any of us of the alleged crimes. I kept waiting and waiting throughout the trial; when are they going to bring in some sort of evidence that was going to be convincing?" Another juror expressed, "I went in there with the courage to convict a celebrity ... and witness after witness, I was more convinced of the innocence." Yet another juror shared, "I can't say that there was anything that convinced me to say guilty, ever, throughout the trial."[343] Jury foreman Paul Rodriguez said, "The more we listened, ... the more we thought that they don't have a case."[344] When the press asked the jurors whose testimony they found credible, the jurors responded, "the telephone people"—in other words, the people reading the call logs from the telephone company.[345]

To bolster their weak case, the police introduced "prior bad acts." They alleged that Michael Jackson had previously molested five other boys. As mentioned earlier, they could not get the 1993 accuser, Jordan Chandler, to testify and cooperate with them. They brought in Jason Francia, the son of a former maid of Michael's, who claimed he had been tickled inappropriately by Michael. The maid had sold her story to the tabloids and sued Michael Jackson, ultimately reaching an out-of-court settlement. The prosecutors then brought in several witnesses with massive credibility issues. Three of these witnesses had worked at Neverland between 1990 and 1994, one of whom swore under oath in 1993 that she saw nothing, and another signed a statement that he saw nothing. After the ranch fired them in 1994, they sold stories to the tabloids and sued Michael Jackson for wrongful termination. They lost that suit, and the court ordered them to pay $1.4 million to Michael Jackson in damages. Michael countersued two of them, and the courts found them guilty of stealing from his property. They never paid the court-ordered money, and at the time of their testimony owed Michael a large sum of cash.[346] Another of the witnesses, not involved in the wrongful termination lawsuit, sold stories to the tabloids and never went to the authorities with her concerns.[347] All of the witnesses had told contradicting and ever-changing stories through the years. The prosecutors brought them in to testify that they had witnessed Michael Jackson molest other boys in the early 1990s. The boys they mentioned were Wade Robson, Macaulay Culkin, and Brett Barnes. The defense, however, brought in all three boys as their first three witnesses, and all three testified that they had not been molested, nor had the prosecution even asked them if they had been molested.

Michael's attorney, Tom Mesereau, said of District Attorney Tom Sneddon:

> His zeal to get Michael Jackson was irrational and cruel. ... I remember when we were about to start the defense case, he asked me, "Who are your first witnesses going to be tomorrow?" and I said, "Wade Robson, Macaulay Culkin, and Brett Barnes." And he looked dumbfounded. ... He just seemed thunderstruck. He leaned on the jury rail. His face was pale. His eyes looked stunned.[348]

Tom Mesereau had considered not putting on a defense at all, as he felt confident that the jury would not convict Michael after the prosecution rested their case. However, he was concerned there might be a hung jury and felt Michael could not take the toll of another potential trial and, as such, proceeded to call defense witnesses.[349]

How did Michael handle the trial? Friend and witness Brett Barnes stated that Michael lost some of the light in his eyes. Brett said, "The accusations, the way it was presented in the media, if that happened to anyone, that has the ability to break a person. ... The energy you saw beforehand, the carefreeness, the sense of adventure, were dulled down. ... It definitely hurt him. ... You could tell he was going through it. ... He was frail."[350]

Bodyguard Kerry Anderson stated of Michael:

> He was not coping with it well at all. It emotionally drained him. He was a broken man. ... They chose a lie that was so ugly. ... He was a very humane, loving, caring person. He cared for his staff. He knew he was responsible for two hundred or three hundred employees and what was happening to his finances because of all this crazy stuff going on. ... So, he cared. That was a concern

of his. ... And people were believing it because it was all on the media. The power of media is amazing. They can take a person like a Michael Jackson, who was a person with morals, scruples, and values, and demonize him into being some kind of satanic child molester. ... It took a toll on him. ... Just being able to wake up and get up and get dressed for court was a demonstration of the strength and the resilience that he had. ... I saw him break down several times on the way to court. ... Emotionally, with tears and crying and fear.[351]

Attorney Tom Mesereau stated that the media made daily efforts to "besmirch, degrade, dehumanize, and mock Michael Jackson." He said of Michael:

Imagine the Michael Jackson you know, extraordinarily sensitive, extraordinarily intuitive, very creative, very humane, very compassionate, a genius who sees things we don't see, who hears things we can't hear, ... so you take someone with that extraordinary sensitivity and throw him into this nightmarish criminal trial, and he's being accused of conspiring with other hoodlums to abduct children, to falsely imprison a family, to take a cancer-stricken child who at one point was thought to be dying and give him alcohol to prepare him to be molested. If you put all these allegations together, they were saying he was a monster. And you take an extraordinarily sensitive, gifted, vulnerable person like that and make him sit there five days a week for five months, not to mention the stressful build-up to the trial, where the media coverage was terrible and every day he knows if these strangers choose to believe the prosecutors and the police, you know, "I'm probably going to die in a California state prison." And you throw in all the horrible stories about what prison life is like. So, you would expect someone like that to have an enormously difficult time coping with it. Any human being, even people with thicker skin and less sensitivity than him, have a hard time. ... I noticed him losing weight, and as we all know, on verdict day, he just looked horrible. He looked like his cheeks were sunken in, he hadn't slept for days, he looked very, very haggard, and very paralyzed with fear. ... I think because of his extraordinarily sensitive being, his extraordinarily kind, decent ways, I think it made it harder for him to sit there day after day and be accused of being a monster that he couldn't even imagine being. ... I think he had bouts of just utter terror. ... He was a sensitive soul not built for this process, and the cruel hoops he was forced to go through to exonerate himself were just unimaginable. ... He was the most unlikely defendant in a criminal case facing charges like this, but there he was.[352]

Investigator Scott Ross recounted:

Michael was not eating. ... He would move very slowly. ... You could see him getting thinner. You could see him deteriorating. You could see his walk was slowing down. ... A lot of that was protected by his mom because of her age, and he would walk arm and arm with his mom; they would walk slowly, and it sort of looked like he was just escorting his mom, and I really believe that his mom was holding him up most of the time. I think she was the one that was escorting Michael. ... It was pretty hard to watch. You're watching someone literally deteriorate before your eyes for some lunatic's ego.[353]

Friend and musical collaborator Brad Buxer stated of the five-month trial, "He was losing weight, not eating, I think he got down to 102 pounds, very dark times, very scary times."[354] Violet Gaitan shared, "It was apparent to everyone during the trial, the physical change that Michael was going through and that was very difficult to see. You could tell he was under tremendous stress, doing his best to be brave and show up every day. I can't imagine what he was going through."[355]

106

Friend David Nordahl recalled that Michael was "devastated, absolutely devastated" and that his primary concern was what would happen to his children if he went to prison. "Never, ever, did he once say, 'What's going to happen to me?'" stated Nordahl.[356] Attorney Tom Mesereau shared how the trial impacted Michael's children, "[They] were crying. They knew something was wrong with their father. He was going through some type of painful ordeal. ... Children are intuitive. They pick up things. It was a very awful experience. It was painful."[357]

Closing arguments were completed on Friday, June 3, 2005. The case had been tried in a very conservative county with a very high conviction rate. Reporter Aphrodite Jones ran into the prosecution team at a restaurant after closing arguments but before the verdict. She spoke of how they were celebrating what they thought was going to be a victory:

> In the restaurant was a special party for the prosecution team. They were sitting at the bar. ... They were having a celebration dinner before the verdict. ... [They] were all having drinks and toasting each other. ... They were extraordinarily self-satisfied with the way the case had gone. ... They were celebrating that night because they were expecting ... [to] put Michael Jackson behind bars.[358]

The headlines in anticipation of the verdict were brutal and cruel. The front page of the *New York Post* taunted Michael with the headline: "Sweat, Freak."

The jury returned with a verdict on Monday, June 13, 2005. Michael Jackson had been charged with fourteen crimes, ranging from conspiracy to molestation to giving alcohol to minors. As such, when he arrived in court on June 13 to listen to the verdicts, it was not one but fourteen verdicts that were read. The entire set of verdicts took close to five minutes to read, undoubtedly an excruciatingly long five minutes for Michael Jackson. All fourteen verdicts came back the same: not guilty. A woman outside the courtroom was holding fourteen white doves in a cage. For each verdict read, she freed one of the white doves into the air.

Michael cried during the reading of the verdict. One of his attorneys, Susan Yu, sobbed. Several female jurors had tears in their eyes as the judge opened the verdict envelopes.[359] When asked afterward why she cried, one of the female jurors explained, "It started because the other lawyer for Michael Jackson [Susan Yu] lost it, when she lost it, I lost it, because … throughout the whole trial, she would just look at the witnesses, not move, she would just stare at them the whole time. … She was always so alert and everything, and then to see, my gosh, her emotions just come pouring out."[360] A few days before the reading of the verdict, Michael confided to Susan, "Suzy, I just want to tell you how grateful I am to God and my family for having found you and Tom. That is the best thing that ever happened to me. I just want to thank you so much for everything you have done." Susan stated of Michael, "He was so decent and so modest and humble."[361] Jury foreman Paul Rodriguez noted that during the reading of the verdict, Michael looked over at the jurors and quietly mouthed "Thank you."[362]

Michael was immensely relieved after the reading of the verdicts, but the mood was not celebratory. Attorney Tom Mesereau stated, "Michael was exhausted. He had trouble even walking. He was so relieved but battered. … The feeling at Neverland was not a celebratory feeling. … It was just, 'Oh my God, thank God it's over.'"[363]

Bodyguard Kerry Anderson recounted:

> Michael was in a state of shock, … he was so emotionally, physically, and mentally messed up, it was not a good day, he was just going through the motions. When somebody guts you, they cut your extremities off and say you're free, you're still numb from that six months … of mental conditioning that they did. It really impacted him. It wasn't celebratory at all on the way home. It was very somber.[364]

Big Al was off work the day of the verdict and rushed to Neverland to greet Michael. He recalled:

> I got in my truck, and I drove like a hundred miles an hour to the ranch because I said there is no way I'm not going to be there when he comes home after all the crap he's been through to show my support. ... All the employees lined the roads coming down that last hill to the gates ... on both sides, there's a hundred of us out there; we're all holding hands, and we greeted him coming back, and that was a pretty special moment for all of us.[365]

Michael had survived the ordeal of his life. Investigative reporter Charles Thomson poignantly shared his thoughts on the trial:

> The victory means nothing; the triumph means nothing or very little if you remove from the equation the struggle that preceded it. The peak is made that much greater when it's compared with the trough. He really almost died during that trial. It's a miracle that he did not die during that trial. The misery and the pain of the injustice that was inflicted upon this man was horrific, and just surviving that makes him a hero. ... They did everything they could to completely destroy this man—the authorities, the government, the media, criminals—did everything they could to completely destroy this man, and he didn't let them.[366]

The trial, under normal circumstances, should never have happened. The timeline was nonsensical. The details of the allegations kept changing. The Arvizos were upset that Michael had distanced himself from them. This anger was not unlike the anger of Evan Chandler when Michael stopped talking to him. The Arvizos had minimal credibility and a history of seeking payment from celebrities and pursuing dubious lawsuits. There was no evidence to support their claims. There was no credible corroborating witness testimony and no physical evidence. Many of the prosecution's witnesses were people with very dubious backgrounds—people who sold stories to the tabloids for compensation and people whom Michael Jackson had successfully sued. Yet, for five months and the two years preceding, beginning with the airing of the Bashir documentary, the press largely spoke of the allegations as if they were fact, as if there was massive evidence to back them up. They put Michael Jackson through hell and smeared his reputation at every opportunity. Even though the allegations were so demonstrably absurd, for two years, Michael had to face the prospect of spending the rest of his life in prison. The way he was treated was cruel and criminal. But the jury saw through it all. They resisted the massive media pressure and acquitted Michael Jackson on all counts.

12

The Recovery

It was never the way it used to be. ... Too much had happened. In terms of the trial, it just knocked the living crap out of him. - Musical collaborator Brad Buxer

After the trial, Michael Jackson did not stay at Neverland for long. His attorney, Tom Mesereau, told him to leave Neverland and never return. Mesereau felt that the prosecutors had been humiliated by the verdict and would be desperate to find another case to pursue Michael with again.[367] Violet Gaitan stated of Michael, "This poor man is never going to come back. He can never live here again. It's never going to be the same. That created a lot of sadness for me. ... Michael injected a spirit into Neverland, and it was a living, breathing thing on its own. And without him, I couldn't see it being the place that it was. It was really hard on us." Gaitan shared that it was very difficult to move on from Neverland because she was so attached to its purpose.[368] Due to both the trial and the financial upkeep of Neverland, it was essentially shut down not long after the verdicts came in. Michael only stayed on the property for a few days and then left, never to return.

And what of the media coverage of the trial? Did they apologize to Michael for their salacious and slanted coverage and explain to audiences how and why they had gotten the case so wrong? No. Instead, they questioned if the jurors had been overwhelmed by Michael's celebrity, clouding their judgment. However, one reporter, Aphrodite Jones, reassessed her prior coverage of the court case. As a reporter for *Fox*, she had been encouraged to focus on the salacious accusations, and she had participated in the unfair reporting of the trial. However, she stated later that when the verdicts came in, it was like a fog lifting. She was able to see clearly finally. She re-looked at the case and concluded that the jury was correct. As someone who had written seven *New York Times* bestsellers, she decided to write a book analyzing the trial. However, no publisher would touch her book. They all gave her the same feedback: They did not want to publish a positive book about Michael Jackson. The book was not even about Michael Jackson. It was simply an analysis of the trial. However, it came to the same conclusion as the jury, and the publishing industry had no interest in that.[369] Because the press never exposed the public to fair trial coverage, many assumed that Michael had "gotten away with it."

After leaving Neverland, Michael briefly visited France and then settled in the Middle Eastern country of Bahrain as a guest of Prince Shiek Abdulla bin Hamad bin Isa Al Khalifa. Michael's bodyguard, Kerry Anderson, went with him. Anderson later reflected on Michael's need to leave the United States, "Michael basically was done with the United States. He didn't believe in the judicial system. He believed that they could do him like this again. And he was very fearful of what could potentially happen again. … You could tell Michael was really in better shape once we got over there [to Bahrain]."[370] While in Bahrain, Michael also visited other nearby countries. His desire to acclimate to the local cultures sometimes made his bodyguard nervous. Anderson recounted one such story:

> When we arrived in Oman, the people that hosted us … certain times of the month, they would go out in the mountains and live without electricity and running water because that was their culture, I guess. And they were explaining that to Michael, and he was like, "Oh, I want to go!" … [I'm thinking] Let's not go in the mountains, let's stay in the city. … It was so mountainous, so far

away from the city; all you see is mountains and caves, and you see a guy walking with a herd of sheep coming down the mountain. To myself, I'm thinking, what are we doing here? I don't like this at all.

Even in these remote areas, however, people would run up to Michael and excitedly exclaim, "Michael Jackson!" Anderson, amazed, thought to himself, "Even these people know this man." Anderson tried to discourage Michael from going on these excursions, but there was no talking him out of it.[371]

Michael's hairstylist, Carol LaMere, stated that after the trial, Michael "was very leery about a lot of things. ... I think he was very hurt. He was very hurt that people would think this of him." Nonetheless, she said she had never seen him so happy and relaxed as he was in the Middle East.[372] After spending approximately one year recuperating in the Middle East, Michael moved on to the Irish countryside, where he stayed for roughly half a year.

While there, he befriended Dr. Patrick Treacy, who echoed many of the same sentiments about Michael that others had expressed over the years:

> The sad fact is you only had to be in his company [for] five minutes, and he emitted this total radiance of goodness. You never really heard him give out about anybody else, and even though he was bothered by a lot of people who I would say were almost stealing from him money-wise, he never really castigated them. ... There was just no badness in him.[373]

During Michael's time in Ireland, there had been an incident where children had suffered horrible burns, and Michael continually asked Dr. Treacy how those children were doing, no doubt remembering his own burns:

> From time to time, you'd be chatting about something else, and he just ... would turn around and say something like, "Patrick, tell

me, are those children in pain now?" ... Three or four days later, it would be back to the same thing. You could see that things like that bothered him continually. There was just genuine affection for other people and, particularly, children.[374]

Dr. Treacy also spoke of Michael's incessant curiosity:

> He was very intelligent. ... He could sit and tell you about Ireland in a way that ... I wouldn't have expected. He'd know about the history surrounding the place he lived back maybe two thousand years. ... Even though I lived in Ireland ... I didn't know that. ... I have a nice library in the clinic, and he often wanted to deprive me of some of my better texts. And the things he would pick out would be about $400 books, and I'd try and replace them with something else and say, "Michael, there's nicer pictures in this one," and he'd look at me and say, "You know I don't fall for that sort of thing, Patrick."[375]

During both his time in the Middle East and in Ireland, Michael continued to work on music, but he did not release any new songs during this period. On November 15, 2006, Michael appeared at the World Music Awards in London, his first public appearance in the West since his acquittal. He had previously appeared at the MTV Japan Legends Awards on May 26, 2006, to receive an award and was visibly touched by the fan reaction. At the World Music Awards in London, he also accepted an award and gave a brief performance. Investigative journalist Charles Thomson was in the crowd:

> When Michael Jackson eventually appeared, the place exploded. I've seen Paul McCartney, I've seen Madonna, I've seen Prince, I've seen George Michael; I've never in my life, before or since, witnessed any artist provoke the response that Michael Jackson provoked that night. He received the most sustained, thunderous reception I've ever seen. ... For the duration of his speeches, I

hardly heard a word he said despite the booming sound system. Most artists receive a big cheer as they walk on stage, and then the audience settles down. Michael provoked hysteria, shrieking, and crying. It didn't lull once from the moment he appeared ... until he disappeared backstage again. ... It was so loud my ears were hurting.[376]

Another member of the audience said it was "absolutely deafening." Michael's photographer, Harrison Funk, stated that he thought the building was going to collapse from all the screaming and stomping. He said, "I was next to audio monitors, and I couldn't hear him speak. ... It was just overrun by cheers." The following morning, many media outlets reported that the audience had booed Michael Jackson off the stage.[377] The video footage of him being wildly cheered on is available today for all to see on YouTube. The false media claims of booing came about because fans booed the singer Rihanna as she came on stage when they had expected Michael instead. The media reports show how grossly the press can misrepresent an event. They also reveal the disdain the press felt towards Michael. But the reaction to his appearance at the World Music Awards conveyed the depth to which much of the public, despite two decades of slander, still loved him.

At the end of 2006, Michael left Ireland and returned to the United States, settling in Las Vegas. When Michael arrived, he was going through a difficult transition phase in his life. He was asset-rich but cash-poor. His most significant asset was his Sony/ATV catalogue (which his estate sold for $750 million after Michael's death). By 2007, he had not performed for some time, and the income coming in from music publishing, both his own and others, was being directed primarily at paying off debts secured against those assets and settling lawsuits. Michael's bodyguards stated that Michael was an "easy target"[378] and always settled lawsuits because he was so traumatized by the 2005 criminal trial that he would do anything to avoid another courtroom.[379]

Despite hesitating to return to the limelight, Michael continued to work on music. However, his musical collaborator, Brad Buxer, said the vibe differed greatly from prior working sessions. "It was never the way it used to be," stated Buxer. "Too much had happened. In terms of the trial, it just knocked the living crap out of him. ... We didn't have a record deal. There was no talk about touring."[380] Javon Beard, one of Michael's bodyguards, stated of Michael, "It just seemed like he had no interest in work or business in general, but he still loved to create, to make music. ... If he talked about music or dancing, it was purely from the creative side. Any time the conversation turned toward the business or commercial side, there was no joy, no enthusiasm." Bill Whitfield, another bodyguard of Michael's, shared, "For the most part, he was just writing and creating music because he loved doing it."[381] The bodyguards said Michael would often be up in the middle of the night, singing in his studio. Beard recalled, "It gave me goosebumps. How could you not get goosebumps hearing Michael Jackson performing like that? In the dead of night, just sitting there and listening by yourself, no one else around? We never really got used to it. It was always amazing no matter how many times we heard it."[382]

In addition to his music, Michael also kept himself busy with his children and his library. He went to Los Angeles and bought out an entire used bookstore and then had all the books shipped to Vegas to create a library in the house. Whitfield shared, "He'd just go in there and get lost and find interesting things to read."[383] Bodyguard Mike Garcia stated, "Because of technology, [Michael] felt libraries would be extinct one day, so we constantly lugged the books around with us. ... You could say the title of the book, or you could say the author of the book ... and he would know exactly what book it was or who the author was. ... He was very intelligent. He absorbed everything."[384] The bodyguards would also regularly bring him all the foreign newspapers they could find, including ones not in English. The only American paper Michael read was the *Wall Street Journal*.[385] His bodyguards indicated that they had heard him speak to fans in French, Spanish, and Japanese.[386]

Michael did not lose his humanitarian spirit during these years. According to his bodyguards, Michael asked them to drive him to the homeless area of Las Vegas, where he slightly rolled down his tinted window, chatted with the homeless individuals, and gave out $100 bills, asking them to use the money to buy something nourishing, not drugs. The homeless never knew it was Michael Jackson they were talking to. One man asked him, "Are you Michael Jackson?" and Michael responded, "No." Other times, he would have his bodyguards drive around these same areas, once with Michael's children, and hand out food.[387] Michael's interest in people experiencing homelessness goes back to at least the early 1980s. Keyboardist Rory Kaplan recounted a story of Michael asking him one night in 1984 when they were performing in Atlanta if he wanted to get out of the hotel. They drove down to the homeless area in the city, and Michael spoke with the individuals on the street and gave them food. Kaplan stated, "There were no cameras rolling. I think Michael religiously thought you have to give back a bit."[388] Michael's son Prince shared what his father taught him:

> As a human being, as part of the human experience, it's important to have others ... acknowledge your existence, and ... if you're down on hard times, and homeless people, whatever issue or whatever reason they are for being homeless, they understand that they are down on hard times, and if you're just out looking for help, in any situation, ... if you were looking for help from a family member, from a friend, from whoever, and they don't even acknowledge that you're there, ... that would hurt a lot, ... and that would make it worse. ... If you can't buy them anything or you don't have any cash to give them, then it's just as simple as looking them in the eye and saying, "I'm sorry, I don't have anything."[389]

Even if one cannot help, it is so important always to acknowledge the suffering of others.

Michael showered attention on his children but could also be strict with them. According to Michael's bodyguards, his children did not fully comprehend how famous their father was.[390] He wanted them to become self-sufficient. When he bought a puppy for his son, Prince, he expected him to pick up after it. Unbeknownst to Michael, Prince was leaving that to the bodyguards. After a short while, they tired of it and just left the dog poop alone. While Michael was in the car, headed to an important business meeting, he asked his bodyguards, "Do you smell that? Why does it smell so horrible in here?" After a little while, they discovered dog poop on Michael's shoes. When Michael got home, Prince got in a lot of trouble. Michael told him the dog was his responsibility, not the bodyguards'. After that, Prince always cleaned up after his dog.[391]

While in Bahrain, Michael had hired for his children a teacher who had traveled with them later to Ireland and the United States. She recalled how she would forget that Michael was famous but that it really dawned on her at the World Music Awards. She described Michael as very thoughtful, intelligent, and funny, with a "heart of gold." She stated he was the "greatest boss" and treated her like a family member. Although she homeschooled Michael's children, he had a classroom set up for them wherever they stayed, and they followed regular school hours.[392] In the summer of 2007, Michael took his kids to the Virginia countryside for a few months, then stayed with some friends in New Jersey before returning to Las Vegas in late 2007.

Michael, for the most part, stayed completely out of the limelight during this period of his life, but he could not entirely escape the child molestation allegations that had caused him so much trauma. One day, while out in public in Virginia, a crowd had gathered around him, and someone from the back of the group yelled, "Fuckin' child molester!" According to Michael's bodyguards, hearing someone call him a child molester would cause Michael to hide in his room and emotionally shut down for at least a week, so they lied to him and told him they had not heard anything.[393] Michael was also traumatized from the media exposure. One day, while privately enjoying a hotel swimming pool, Michael saw a video camera; even though the hotel had shut off the camera, he was so distraught he pulled it off the wall and broke it, bloodying his hands. He yelled at the broken camera, "I hate you! I hate you!" The hotel forced him to pay for the broken camera.[394]

Despite the lousy incidents, there were many happy times during these years. Bodyguard Mike Garcia recalled, "His spirit was delightful, ... so positive. ... He was so full of life." He would play pranks on his bodyguards, once giving them an extraordinarily spicy chicken lunch to see how they would react.[395] He also loved to do magic tricks. Bodyguard Bill Whitfield recounted, "He would do magic at the worst damn time sometimes. We're at a hotel. We've got a whole bunch of fans screaming, cameras, media, ... and we're trying to keep people back ... and he'll say, 'Bill, watch this,' ... and [he'll] make a quarter disappear." Whitfield would think to himself, "This is not the time for this," but Michael was so used to the chaos around him that he would act as if nothing was happening.[396]

Although Michael had tried to separate himself from the commercial music industry, by late 2008, he had to make a decision: he could either start selling his assets—which would pay off all his debts and leave him with several hundred million dollars to retire with—or go back to work and pay off his debts without the need to sell assets. He chose the latter. Finances were likely not the only factor. He expressed that he wanted his children to see him perform while he was still young enough to do so, and he also wanted to do it as a thank you to the fans who had supported him through his child molestation trial. According to Michael's primary care physician, Dr. Allan Metzger, Michael was "terribly hurt about the trial and allegations" and wanted to come back into the public arena "in a good light" and "redeem" his name.[397]

Thus, Michael moved to Los Angeles in late 2008 with plans to embark on comeback concert performances. Performances by Michael Jackson were always highly lucrative, and everyone wanted a piece of the pie. Michael told his bodyguards, "The vultures, they're going to start coming now. Everybody is going to want something, and nobody is going to trust anybody else. You're about to see the ugliness in people. Just wait."[398]

13

Michael's Passing

He talked about all the positives and all the things he loved about touring. And then he said something very cryptic. He said, "The only thing I don't like about touring is all the doctors." - Studio engineer Michael Prince

On January 28, 2009, Michael Jackson signed an agreement with AEG Live to perform a series of concerts at London's O2 Arena. The contract was for a minimum of eighteen shows and a maximum of thirty-one. If ticket demand warranted more than thirty-one shows, the parties agreed that AEG would secure Michael's approval before putting them on sale. Michael would receive 90 percent of the tour profits but was responsible for 95 percent of the production costs. AEG would pay for the production costs upfront but would ultimately deduct them from Michael's earnings.[399] While the parties did not sign a contract for a world tour, they discussed that if the concerts in London went well, a world tour would likely follow.

A press conference was scheduled for March 5 at London's O2 Arena for Michael to announce he would be performing ten shows. It is typical industry practice to under-announce what an artist has agreed to. Michael arrived in London on March 3 for the announcement; however, on the day of, he hesitated to make the public appearance. AEG Live CEO Randy Phillips went to Michael's hotel suite to push him to go. Phillips emailed his boss,

AEG President Tim Leiweke: "I screamed so loud the walls are shaking. … This is the scariest thing I have ever seen. He's an emotionally paralyzed mess. … He is scared to death. Right now, I just want to get through this press conference."[400] Phillips likely did not understand the depth of Michael's trauma over his 2005 trial and the brutal media beating he took. The last time Michael was in front of so many press cameras was during that trial. And the cameras were not kind to him then. Michael may have felt ready to perform for his fans and children but appeared unprepared to return to the public sphere. It is understandable why AEG wanted Michael to announce the concerts himself; but from Michael's perspective, he was once again to face countless cameras flashing in his face, and the last time he'd met that, it was the most traumatic experience of his life. By returning to the public spotlight, Michael was once again exposing himself to potential brutal press coverage, and he'd barely survived the last time around.

Michael ultimately arrived at the O2 arena, albeit ninety minutes later than initially scheduled. Approximately 3,000 fans and 350 reporters were waiting for him.[401] The fans were ecstatic when he arrived. His appearance was brief, but it was official: Michael Jackson was returning to the stage.

The following morning, fans were invited to pre-register for tickets on a newly created website called michaeljacksonlive.com. The site struggled with the website traffic, as 1.6 million people pre-registered. Only those who pre-registered were allowed to purchase tickets when the Ticketmaster presale began. Based on the number of people who pre-registered, AEG put up thirty shows as part of the presale instead of the announced ten. They sold out within minutes, causing the Ticketmaster website to crash.[402] Randy Phillips testified that based on that initial demand, AEG believed they could sell out over two hundred shows in London.[403] AEG then asked Michael if he would be willing to perform additional concerts. He agreed to fifty, with the condition that AEG would find him an estate in the countryside to lease with "running streams" and "horses." He did not want to be cooped up in a hotel suite for an extended period. He wanted to live in the countryside.

He also asked that a representative from Guinness World Records appear at the last show.[404] All fifty shows were sold out within hours, making it the fastest-selling concert series in history.[405] The tickets sold essentially as quickly as the computer could process them. Many who tried to purchase tickets were unable to. Five hundred twenty-five thousand people were left waiting in the cue, unable to secure tickets.[406] Phillips said he had never seen that kind of demand. It was unprecedented.[407] This ticket demand occurred shortly after the 2008 financial crisis when discretionary spending was at a low, and most individuals were cautious with their money, further emphasizing just how great the desire was to watch Michael perform.

Many rumors circulated that Michael had not agreed to do fifty shows and that his manager approved the extra dates without informing him. According to the British tabloid *The Sun*, Michael was quoted as telling fans, "I only wanted to do ten and take the tour around the world to other cities, not fifty in one place. I went to bed knowing I sold ten dates and woke up to the news I was booked to do fifty." Others denied these claims. A source close to the negotiations stated, "We couldn't have gone ahead with adding more shows, for a total of fifty, without his direct approval. And he wasn't pissed; there was no happier human being in the world because, to him, it showed people still loved him."[408]

The truth likely lies somewhere in the middle. No doubt Michael was flattered that the demand was so great. But he was likely also, to some extent, daunted by the number of shows. He was now fifty years old. Many of his songs involved intense dance routines. While the performances were never scheduled for two nights in a row, many were scheduled only two days apart, giving Michael only one night of rest in between. It would have been a grueling set of performances. It was also a quick decision that needed to be made, leaving little time for Michael to think through what he was agreeing to. His excitement over the high demand may have contributed to his making a decision that, perhaps given time to reflect, he would not have made. However, he did limit the sales to fifty concerts when the demand was far greater, so he knew he had limitations regarding what his body could handle.

The first show was scheduled for mid-July. It was originally set for July 8 but then moved to July 13. This did not leave much time for preparation. Michael's concerts were always extremely physically demanding. He would perform at full intensity for two to three hours. His primary care physician, Dr. Allan Metzger, testified that he weighed Michael before and after a performance. On average, Michael lost seven or eight pounds during each performance from profusive sweating. Metzger weighed Michael to stress to him how important it was to get fluids back into his body.[409] Indeed, Michael often received fluids via IVs to rehydrate after performing.[410] Exhaustion was another health challenge Michael faced. Guitarist Jennifer Batton shared, "I remember on the *HIStory* tour he had oxygen in his tent where he would breathe oxygen to help him keep going because it would kill most people what he did aerobically."[411]

Sleep while performing was Michael's most considerable difficulty. Dr. Metzger testified that Michael had a "profound sleep disorder." Over the years, Michael had tried various herbal remedies, such as melatonin and echinacea, as well as standard sleep pharmaceuticals. Dr. Metzger stated that such treatments were sufficient for Michael during "uncritical times, when things were not going on emotionally or physically," but "if he was doing an album, if he was performing, under stress for trial, God only knows what he needed for sleep."[412] In the spring of 2009 Michael was not only preparing for a series of demanding concerts, he was also working on new music for an upcoming album, and mentally and emotionally preparing for a return to the spotlight. This was an intense time for him physically, creatively, and psychologically.

When asked about the source of Michael's sleep disorder, Dr. Metzger testified: "I always related it to him being a creative force in the universe, not being happy with certain things coming out of the press, not being happy with a project or something he was working on, and he was dedicated to making it better, always, and always thinking or up at night drawing or something."[413]

Others echoed similar sentiments. Studio engineer Michael Prince said of Michael, "He had this artistic streak in him that didn't stop. ... He had ideas coming into his head all the time."[414] Friend David Nordahl shared, "Michael, ever since I've met him [in 1988], has had problems with sleep. He has such an active mind, and it's hard for him to just lay down and turn that off. It keeps running, all the time."[415] Nordahl also expressed that stress was a contributing factor, "With all the worries and concerns and everything leading up to that trial. Just the letdown from everything that had happened in his life and how he's portrayed and everything. That wore on him even more, and that contributed to his inability to sleep."[416]

Dr. Charles Czeisler, a sleep expert at the Harvard Medical School, testified to the negative effects that performance, and night work in general, can have on a person's sleep cycle:

> The nature of performing late in the day so that—you know, the average performer will tell me, whether performing at a basketball game or performing at a concert, that if—first of all, you can't usually have dinner before you do a major performance or before an NBA game or before a hockey game, so they're all keyed up for that activity. Even the average nightshift worker, when they work, let's say, the 4:00 p.m. to midnight shift, universally they report they can't just go home and go to sleep because they are keyed up from work, whether they're making tires for Michelin tire company or producing a paper or working for a utility. And typically, the average dayshift worker finishes at 5:00, winds down in the evening, has time to relax, watch some television, whatever they're going to do, and it's many hours before they actually then wind down and go to bed, whereas an evening shift worker, when

125

they finish at midnight, it takes them at least a couple of hours after they get home before they can wind down and go to bed.[417]

Michael's makeup artist, Karen Faye, testified, "What would happen is his adrenaline would pump through his body. He would do a two-hour or longer show, and his adrenaline level was so high that it took him at least twenty-four hours to relax and be able to sleep. Sometimes it would take him two days."[418]

In late January, Michael asked Dr. Cherilyn Lee to assist him with the physical demands he was about to undertake. Dr. Lee was a holistic healthcare practitioner with a PhD in holistic nutrition. She met with him more than twenty times over the next three months. She recalled that both he and his home were very warm. "You can walk into a house, and if a person has been arguing in the house, or whatever, you can feel the coldness and feel the tension there. When you walk into his house, you just feel love. You feel a warmth, you feel a love. And being in his presence, that's what you would see, what you would feel. ... He was the most down-to-earth person that I ever met," she said. Michael told her, "I want to use my music to heal people and to heal the world, just like you use your clinic to help heal people." Dr. Lee stated that Michael was more "caring" and "giving" than anyone she had ever met. He often asked her how her other patients were doing and if there was anything he could do to help. She said she had never had a patient concerned about her other patients. She shared that Michael "really cared for people" and would also often ask about her mother, who was not doing well at the time.[419]

During their first meeting, Michael informed Dr. Lee that he was tired and looking for energy through nutrition and food. He told her the only medication he was actively taking was Tylenol PM for insomnia and that he was "very concerned about being healthy." He also informed her that he could lose up to five pounds from heavy sweating during rehearsal. To address his issues, she made him nutrient-loaded smoothies specifically targeted at his nutritional needs and deficiencies. She also gave him vitamins via IV, including vitamin C.[420]

In March, Michael informed Dr. Lee that he needed more help with sleep. He told her that when he's in rehearsal or planning for a concert, he puts so much energy into what he's doing that it's hard for him just to turn everything off and go to sleep at night.[421] She set him up on a plan of natural supplements and herbal teas. He told her he didn't think it would work but would try it anyway. She also discussed sleep hygiene with him. She described sleep hygiene as the sleep environment, such as "going to bed with too much light on, maybe too much music, EMFs [electromagnetic frequencies]." Michael told her, however, that he needed the TV or music on, or he could not sleep at all, implying that his insomnia was likely at least partly psychological. If it were his thoughts that were keeping him awake, then it would make sense that he would want music or the TV on as a distraction.[422]

By mid-April, Dr. Lee suggested they do a sleep study, as nothing was helping and the most Michael could sleep was five hours; but Michael expressed that he needed a more immediate solution and did not have the luxury of time for an extensive study. He said his tour was about to start. During the three months Dr. Lee spent with Michael, she stated that his stress and anxiety increased as time went on. On the morning of April 19, Michael asked Dr. Lee about using propofol for sleep. She had never heard of it, but he told her they used it for surgeries and in dental offices.[423] Michael told her he had been given propofol before but did not mention whether he had used it for sleep.

Later, in court, it was alleged that Michael had been given propofol to sleep during his 1996–1997 *HIStory* tour in between concerts. However, the testimony between various witnesses was not consistent. Debbie Rowe, who bore Michael's first two children, testified that as far as she was aware, he had been given propofol twice to sleep between concerts in Munich and that this was set up by Michael's primary care physician, Dr. Metzger. She had spoken to Dr. Metzger about it, and he informed her it was not his first choice, but nothing else was working and it was only a temporary solution.[424] Metzger, however, denied ever arranging for Michael to be given propofol.[425] Another doctor testified that Michael had told him that he had used propofol on many occasions to sleep during his tours.[426]

Michael himself stated during an interview when asked how he found out about Princess Diana's death, "I woke up, and my doctor gave me the news, and I fell back down in grief."[427] Princess Diana died while Michael was on his *HIStory* tour. Whether Michael was taking propofol in this case is unclear, but his answer implies that he was using doctors to help him sleep on that tour. Shortly before announcing his comeback concerts, Michael told studio engineer Michael Prince how excited he was about returning to the stage. "He talked about all the positives and all the things he loved about touring," stated the engineer, "And then he said something very cryptic. He said, 'The only thing I don't like about touring is all the doctors.' ... It was something I was unaware of, but I am now."[428]

There is no doubt that Michael loved performing. When talking about what it was like to share his music with an audience, he stated, "It's just full of love, it's very emotional, it brings me to tears. ... [I feel] connected to a higher force, and you become one with the spirit ... It's very spiritual."[429] However, there was also a dark side to performing. Dr. Lee testified about that morning of April 19, when Michael asked her about propofol and told her he was "very tired." She stated:

> He seemed very—he seemed like something was going on, other than—he wasn't quite him—I mean, [typically] he was very jovial, very happy, very up, but that morning, he just didn't kind of seem that way. I remember being in his bedroom, and I could look out the window and see the kids outside under the tree, and he just wasn't quite—we had lunch that day too, and—but he wasn't quite himself. Not himself. He just seemed really stressed or something.

He said at certain points, he was just under a lot of pressure to finish up, finish rehearsals and stuff. And he said, "I've got to get a good night's sleep so I can do this. I've got to get a good night's sleep."[430]

Michael agreed to have Dr. Lee stay overnight on the evening of April 19 so she could watch him sleep and give advice on what he may be doing incorrectly. She then went to study what propofol was, and when she returned that night, she told Michael it was dangerous, not meant to treat insomnia, and should never be taken in the home. She described all the potential side effects to him. Michael responded that doctors had told him it was safe as long as he was monitored. He told Dr. Lee that she could stay overnight every night with the doctor to ensure he was administering it appropriately. Dr. Lee broke down in tears in court as she recounted that evening:

> We went back and forth for a few minutes because he was very persistent to try to explain to me how "I'm going to be safe." … And I could feel where he was coming from because the doctors will put people on medication and tell them, "You will be safe." I hear it all the time, from my cancer patients to the chemo—this is something I hear all the time. So, I could feel where he was coming from. … So that's why I was trying to tell him how it wasn't safe, but if doctors have already told him it was safe, and your doctor has told you it's safe—this is one reason why I couldn't even help my own mother. … I kept telling her she couldn't take all this medication, and she did, and she died … because she believed her doctor.[431]

Unable to convince Michael, she then stayed overnight to monitor his sleep. He slept approximately three hours and then was wide awake. She said Michael was very "agitated" when he woke up. He complained that he had a huge day of rehearsal in front of him and could not rehearse unless he slept. He said, "I only have a little time left for rehearsal, and I need to sleep all night. I have to sleep all night."[432] Dr. Lee testified that Michael seemed desperate and was very sincere and earnest in his belief that doctors had told him propofol was safe.

In late April, Michael stopped seeing Dr. Lee, and by early May, Michael began treatment with Dr. Conrad Murray for his insomnia. Michael had first met Murray a couple of years prior in Las Vegas when Murray treated Michael's children for an illness. The exact date Michael began receiving propofol is unknown, but it is estimated to have been near the start of May. On May 6, AEG verbally agreed with Dr. Conrad Murray to hire him for the upcoming tour, at Michael's request, at $150,000 monthly. AEG would pay Murray, but the cost would come from Michael's profits.[433] AEG began working on a contract between themselves and Dr. Murray, which would also require Michael's signature. At the time of Michael's death, neither AEG nor Michael had yet signed the contract, so Murray was never paid for his services.

Michael's eldest son, Prince, testified that he would see Dr. Lee downstairs with his father, giving him vitamins via an IV. At some point, Dr. Lee stopped coming, and he started seeing Dr. Murray downstairs with his father, also giving him an IV of clear liquid, which Prince assumed was vitamins as that is what Dr. Lee had been giving his father. Then, at some point, Dr. Murray began treating his father upstairs.[434]

In addition to being treated for dehydration and insomnia, Michael also brought on a personal trainer and a chef to help prepare him for his tour. Lou Ferrigno came on as Michael's trainer. Ferrigno had trained Michael on and off for fifteen years. He only worked with Michael through the latter part of May and planned to return and do a few more sessions with him before Michael left for London. Ferrigno stated that when he last saw Michael, Michael still looked great.[435] He was "energetic," "happy," "lean," "animated," and "always talking about nutrition."[436] Michael told his chef, Kai Chase, "I know you're good at what you do. ... I need you to feed me healthy." Chase would regularly feed Michael organic vegetables, fish, organic lean meats (chicken and turkey), and organic vegetable juices.[437]

It was not just his body but also the entire concert production that Michael Jackson needed to prepare. The show was an elaborate event that included dancers, musicians, backup singers, sophisticated staging, and special effects. While Michael performed one-off shows in the late 1990s and early 2000s, his last concert tour had been in 1996–1997. Thus, he needed to rely on many new faces to fill out the team, but some familiar ones also returned. Michael asked Kenny Ortega to direct the show. Ortega had previously worked with Michael on his *HIStory* and *Dangerous* tours in the 1990s.

Rehearsals began in late March 2009 in Los Angeles. The overall feedback from those working with Michael on his upcoming concerts was that he was very excited about returning to the stage. He shared with everyone:

> It's an adventure; it's a great adventure. It's nothing to be nervous about. They just want wonderful experiences. They want escapism. We want to take them places that they've never been before. We want to show them talent that they've never seen before. So, give your all. And I love you all. We're a family, just know that. We're a family. We have to bring love back into the world, to remind the world that love is important ... love each other. We're all one. That's the message. And take care of the planet. ... We have an important message.[438]

Backup singer Judith Hill stated of Michael:

> He was so connected to using music as a vehicle to really heal the world. And I think he really did that with his music. I remember being in rehearsals and feeling stuff that I never really felt before in that capacity and realizing what a service he had given to the world. That these weren't just incredible songs and productions; this is

Michael's way really of helping people, and healing people, and touching people's hearts with his music, and realizing just exactly what he was doing. He wasn't just the greatest pop star and the greatest performer; it was more than that. It was about his desire to heal the world with love and to really write music that touches at the deepest core of a human level. And so I think walking away from those rehearsals really gave me a sense of the gravity of what he was doing. Before, I was just a fan, and I just loved his music, and I thought he was just so insanely incredible. But coming out of those rehearsals, you just really feel something so powerful and so important about the mission and his calling on this planet.[439]

Choreographer Travis Payne shared what Michael had confided in him, "He told me, 'I can go do a news conference and tell people statistics, ... but people don't listen; you have to put it in a song, you have to affect people on a physiological level, you have to get it into their consciousness, then they will act.'"[440]

Michael had a clear vision of the messages he wanted to promote with his concert series. Michael knew his music well, so the concert rehearsals were mainly to get all the other performers and crew ready and to ensure all could perform cohesively with Michael and with each other. Michael was very supportive of those who would be performing with him. Backup singer Judith Hill shared:

He was just a sweetheart. He was really this very kind, warm-spirited person. Shy, but shy to us, his new band, but really grateful to us. Incredibly kind and grateful and just almost like a kid in a playground. Really whimsical. Really just a pleasant person to be around. And very encouraging at the same time. He was always about letting us know how appreciated we were. So, I thought that was just really awesome of him.[441]

While Michael was enjoying the process of creating the show and getting ready to get back on stage, the physical demands on him were becoming overwhelming. To respond to these demands, he enlisted Dr. Murray to help ensure he was rested, a tragic mistake. By all accounts, Michael was fit and healthy in April. However, starting in May and then, especially in June, he began to lose a lot of weight, and his health started to deteriorate noticeably. Michael also began to miss rehearsals. The director, Kenny Ortega, was frustrated because he could not prepare the show if Michael was not there.[442] Michael knew well what he needed to do, but the others needed his help to prepare. So Ortega emailed AEG executive Paul Gongaware on June 14:

> Were you aware that MJ's doctor didn't permit him to attend rehearsals yesterday? ... Who is responsible for MJ getting proper nourishment/vitamins/therapy every day? Personally, I feel he should have a top nutritionist and physical therapist working with him on a regular basis. The demands on this guy are mentally and physically extraordinary! The show requirements exhaust our 20-year-olds. Please don't underestimate the need to stay on top of this.[443]

Gongaware responded within the hour, stating that he'd requested a face-to-face meeting with Dr. Murray for the following day, and writing, "We want to remind him [Dr. Murray] that it is AEG, not MJ, who is paying his salary. We want him to understand what is expected of him."[444] This email implies that AEG viewed Murray as responsible for ensuring Michael could rehearse. This is not the same as ensuring Michael was healthy. AEG had invested over $30 million in these concerts.[445] That investment depended on Michael's ability to perform. And while Michael's health and ability to perform may seem to have been one and the same, they were not necessarily so. The arrangement between AEG, Conrad Murray, and Michael Jackson was rife with conflicts of interest. Each of the three parties had an interest in Michael being able to perform: AEG, because of the funds they had invested in the concerts; Murray because his continued employment depended on Michael performing; and Michael himself because he very much wanted to have great performances and redeem his tarnished image. Therefore, what was best for Michael's genuine health was bound to get lost in these conflicts of interest, even if all three parties genuinely desired that Michael be healthy.

Michael's son Prince testified that his father was very excited about the concerts but that the demanding rehearsal schedule caused him much anxiety, "He would get off the phone. He would cry sometimes. … After he got off the phone with them, he would cry. … He would say, 'They're going to kill me, they're going to kill me.'" He said his father was particularly stressed after conversations with AEG Live CEO Randy Phillips. When Prince was asked if his father fought back, he replied, "No. My dad didn't fight. He was like my grandma. He was too kind to fight anybody." Prince further testified that Phillips would arrive at his house unannounced when his father was not there. He saw him speaking with Murray twice in his father's absence, including on the evening before his father's death, in hushed whispers, grabbing his elbow, making hand motions, and looking aggressive. Murray arrived at the house regularly in the evenings while Michael was still at rehearsal, and that is when Phillips met with him. One evening Prince called his father to tell him Phillips was at the house, and that is the last conversation he ever had with his dad.[446]

Michael's chef, Kai Chase, testified that she had witnessed Murray storm out of a meeting with AEG executives and mutter, "I can't take this shit."[447]

The concern over Michael's health came to a head on the night of June 19. Michael arrived at rehearsals but was in no shape to perform. He had horrible flu-like symptoms and seemed mentally not all there. Ortega felt perhaps there was not just something physical, but also psychological, that was the source of Michael's troubles that evening. Ortega, concerned, emailed CEO Randy Phillips after the rehearsal finished:

Michael appeared quite weak and fatigued this evening. He had a terrible case of the chills, was trembling, rambling, and obsessing. Everything in me says he should be psychologically evaluated. If we have any chance at all to get him back in the light, it's going to take a strong therapist to help him through this, as well as immediate physical nurturing. I was told by our Choreographer that during the Artist's costume fitting with his Designer tonight, they noticed he's lost more weight. As far as I can tell, there is no one taking responsibility (caring for) him on a daily basis. Where was his assistant tonight? Tonight, I was feeding him, wrapping him in blankets to warm his chills, massaging his feet to calm him, and calling his doctor. There were four security guards outside his door, but no one offering him a cup of hot tea. Finally, it's important for everyone to know, I believe that he really wants this. It would shatter him, break his heart if we pulled the plug. ... He was like a lost boy. There still may be a chance he can rise to the occasion if we get him the help he needs.[448]

Stage Manager John Hougdahl sent a similar email to Phillips that same evening. In his email, he wrote, "I have watched him deteriorate in front of my eyes over the last eight weeks. ... He used to do multiple 360 spins back in April. He'd fall on his ass if he tried now."[449]

Ortega expressed that he felt the issue might have been emotional because he sensed there were more than just physical symptoms that were troubling Michael. Ortega did not know what the problem was, but he felt it was more than just a bad flu, and he did not think it was drug-related in any way.[450] He later testified, "[Michael] wasn't right; he wasn't well, there was something going on. It was deeply troubling me. ... He appeared lost and a little incoherent. ... I did feel that he was not well at all. ... He just seemed ... [like] he wasn't there. There was just something wrong." Ortega said he had never seen Michael like that before.[451] Michael's makeup artist, Karen Faye, testified of that day that Michael "was cold as ice cubes. He was shivering and shaking and couldn't get warm." She stated that Michael kept repeating himself and she had never seen him in that state in all the years she had worked with him.[452]

Michael's chef, Kai Chase, testified:

> Mr. Jackson, with his rehearsals and his schedule, I could see that it was taking a toll on him. And one day, I did observe his son Prince, the eldest, actually having to help him up the stairs into the den area where the children would play. At that point, he looked very thin; he looked very weak. And for a twelve-year-old to be trying to carry his father into an area to still play with them like they used to, what they used to do back in April, it saddened me, and I knew that I had to get this man as healthy as possible, but I did not know why he was deteriorating this way.

> ... I felt that it was strange that there was a doctor there but [Michael was] slowly deteriorating. I didn't understand that.[453]

Chase also found it strange that Dr. Murray did not seem to take an interest in Michael's overall well-being: "For a doctor to have a patient there, and you don't consult with their chef of [sic] eating habits or nutrition? It was quite strange to me. I'd asked him a couple of times, but his answer to me would always be, 'You can fix him anything.'"[454]

Prince testified of his father's condition in the last few weeks of his life, "Some days he would come downstairs and say he's freezing cold, and it was during the summer, so I didn't know why he was so cold. And some days, he would say he's hot. ... His temperature, body temperature was up and down."[455]

Phillips responded to Ortega's email of concern on the morning of June 20:

Kenny, it is critical that neither you, me, or anyone around this show become amateur psychiatrists or physicians. I had a lengthy conversation with Dr. Murray, who I am gaining immense respect for as I get to deal with him more. He said that Michael is not only physically equipped to perform and, that discouraging him to, will hasten his decline instead of stopping it. Dr. Murray also reiterated that he is mentally able to and was speaking to me from the house where he had spent the morning with MJ. This doctor is extremely successful (we check everyone out) and does not need this gig, so he [is] totally unbiased and ethical. It is critical that we surround Mike with love and support and listen to how he wants to get ready for July 13. You cannot imagine the harm and ramifications of stopping this show now. It would far outweigh "calling this game in the 7th inning." I am not just talking about AEG's interests here, but the myriad of stuff and lawsuits swirling around MJ that I crisis manage every day and also his well-being. … Enough alarms have sounded. It is time to put out the fire, not burn the building down.[456]

On Saturday, June 20, Ortega and Phillips met with Dr. Murray and Michael. Murray was accusatory towards Ortega and angry at him for not allowing Michael to rehearse the prior evening. Murray told him to stop being an amateur doctor and psychologist and just be the director and leave Michael's health to him.[457] Ortega, on the other hand, could not understand how Michael's health could be deteriorating if he had a doctor who was supposedly taking care of him full time.[458]

Ortega suggested at the meeting that Michael take a few days off and return to rehearsal on June 23.[459] On Sunday, June 21, Michael reached out to Dr. Lee, the holistic healthcare practitioner whom he had worked with in February through April. Michael's assistant called Dr. Lee, but she could hear Michael in the background. Michael was saying, "Please tell her that one side of my body is hot, and one side of my body is cold." Michael wanted her to come see him. She said he sounded scared and frightened.[460] Dr. Lee remembered those symptoms as being side effects of propofol. She felt maybe Michael was calling her for help because he remembered her reading them to him.[461] She was out of town, however, and told Michael's assistant that she would come and see Michael when she returned to Los Angeles; but in the meantime, Michael should be taken to the hospital.[462] No one, however, took him to the hospital. The fact that Michael reached out to Dr. Lee for help after she had admonished him for his interest in propofol implies that perhaps he was starting to realize that he'd made a mistake. One does not usually reach out for help from someone who has castigated them unless they've come to realize that perhaps that someone was correct.

When Michael returned to rehearsals on Tuesday, June 23, it was as though a miracle had happened. He gave an incredible performance, and everyone was shocked at the drastic transformation from only a few days prior. Ortega testified:

> It was miraculous. ... I didn't ask questions. I was just overjoyed at his energy, his state of mind, his enthusiasm. ... He seemed healthy and ready and happy, and there didn't seem to be any leftover issues from the nineteenth. ... I think we all were just so delighted, the energy in the room changed, the hope returned, and it was a gladness and energy in the room that was real positive and optimistic.

Ortega stated that the improvement in Michael in those few days was "extraordinary."[463] He was asked in court about Michael's sudden transformation:

> Attorney: Was it clear to you that on the twenty-third, something had drastically changed?

> Ortega: It was clear to everybody.

Attorney: And you had no idea what could have happened? Like divine intervention?

Ortega: I doubted myself. I remember going, "Did I see something that couldn't have been there?" ... because Michael just didn't seem like the Michael that I had seen on the nineteenth. He was raring to go, fired up, in charge.

Attorney: Was there, in your mind, something that had been done or occurred that changed Michael?

Ortega: Nothing that I could ... conceive of.[464]

The following evening, Wednesday, June 24, Michael gave another excellent performance. Ortega felt everything was back on track, and they would be ready for the London shows on time. The last song that Michael performed on the night of the twenty-fourth was "Earth Song," after which he watched the band perform "Heal the World."[465] By all accounts, Michael Jackson was very happy on the evenings of June 23 and 24. Indeed, in the released rehearsal footage, Michael can be seen smiling after performing. On June 25, Dr. Lee was back in Los Angeles and scheduled to go to Michael's house to help him with his health concerns. Michael's desire to see Dr. Lee indicates that perhaps he was having second thoughts about the propofol. But it was too late. On the morning of June 25, Michael Jackson passed away.

Sleep medicine expert Dr. Charles Czeisler gave a detailed analysis of what he believed was happening to Michael's health during the last two months of his life. He explained that when doctors give anesthesia, they often tell the patient they are putting them to sleep, but that is a very misleading way of explaining what is happening. There is a lot that occurs when one is genuinely asleep. The brain needs sleep because sleep repairs and maintains the neurons in the brain. Dr. Czeisler explained in his testimony:

Genuine sleep dissipates the sleep drive. Propofol anesthesia dissipates the sleep drive. Genuine sleep fulfills the biological need for sleep; propofol does not fulfill the biological need for sleep. So, it would be like eating some sort of cellulose pellets instead of dinner, and your stomach might be full, you would no longer be hungry, but you would have had zero calories, and it would not fulfill any of your nutritional needs.[466]

Dr. Czeisler explained that the symptoms that others testified to witnessing in Michael, such as weight loss, drier skin, body temperature issues, repeating oneself, anxiety, paranoia, slowness in grasping new material, and memory problems (Michael, for the first time, forgot some of the lyrics to his songs) were all symptoms of extreme sleep deprivation. Dr. Czeisler expounded:

With total sleep deprivation over weeks, what actually happens is a loss of weight and a wasting and inability to thermal regulate. The body temperature goes down. There's confusion and difficulty with balance that one would expect with total sleep deprivation, difficulty with memory, the symptom of paranoia with total sleep deprivation, and anxiety. The constellation of symptoms [in Michael Jackson] are consistent with ones I'd imagine would occur with total sleep deprivation.[467]

In April, Michael was in good shape and, by all accounts, healthy, alert, and sharp. By the end of June, he was far too thin and far less mentally sharp. What then of the miraculous recovery on June 23 and 24? It is believed that Michael did not receive any propofol during the few days he had off between June 19 and June 23. Dr. Czeisler explained that the miraculous recovery that everyone attested to was the result of Michael getting genuine sleep. Studies have shown that severely sleep-deprived animals suffer many of the same symptoms that Michael Jackson did, but if they are allowed to sleep for just a few days, they quickly recover and heal. Hence, with just a few days of sleep, Michael Jackson was able to perform once again at a top-notch level.

However, Michael was not afforded a few days off between every rehearsal. The rehearsals were to resume daily, and he once again would have no time to calm down his adrenaline levels after performing. Therefore, Dr. Murray gave him propofol again on the night of June 24. Michael was scheduled to see Dr. Lee on June 25. Perhaps this time, she would have convinced him to stop taking propofol. But it was too late.

Dr. Czeisler testified that even if Murray had properly monitored Michael while giving him propofol, had he continued to administer it nightly without giving Michael time to recover with genuine sleep, Michael would have died of sleep deprivation after approximately eighty days. He made this estimate based on animal studies.[468]

It was revealed in court that Dr. Murray spent the morning of June 25 on his phone, receiving and making various calls and checking emails. He was clearly not paying the required attention to Michael Jackson. Nor did he have the proper monitoring equipment or the proper resuscitation equipment. Most egregious of all, he did not call 911 upon discovering something was wrong with Michael. It can be surmised that Murray first realized something was wrong with Michael shortly after 11:51 a.m. He was on the phone with a female friend of his, and she testified that after a few minutes, she heard coughing. Then Murray never came back on the phone.[469] Somewhere between 12:05 and 12:15, Murray came frantically down into the kitchen and yelled to Kai Chase, the chef, "Get security! Get Prince!" He did not tell her what was wrong or ask her to call 911. Since she was closer to Prince, she went and got him.[470] At 12:13 p.m., Murray called Michael's assistant, Michael Amir Williams, and left a voicemail indicating Michael had a bad reaction and to call him back immediately. He did not tell Williams to call 911. Williams returned Murray's call at 12:15 p.m., and Murray told him to get to the house right away and send someone upstairs. He again did not tell him to call 911. Williams asked the security guards stationed outside the house to go inside and go upstairs. He told them he did not know what was happening, but something was wrong with Michael.[471] Security guard

Alberto Alvarez arrived upstairs shortly before 12:20 p.m. Michael's two oldest children also went upstairs, but the security guards ushered them back downstairs. The children were crying and screaming. Murray asked Alvarez to put some medical supplies in a bag. Alvarez thought Murray was asking him to do this in preparation for going to the hospital. Alvarez then called 911 at 12:20 p.m., almost a full half hour after Murray first realized something was wrong with Michael.[472] Every medical expert who testified at Conrad Murray's criminal trial stated that his waiting to call 911 was unconscionable. Had Murray called 911 immediately, Michael would have survived. Murray was ultimately convicted of involuntary manslaughter and sentenced to four years in prison and released on parole after two.

During Murray's court case, it was revealed that he had secretly recorded Michael Jackson on the night of May 10. Michael was speaking in a highly drugged and slurred state. The judge referred to the recording as Murray's "insurance policy." In other words, if the relationship between Michael and Murray turned sour or if Michael decided he did not want Murray's services anymore, Murray could blackmail him with the tape or sell it to the media.[473] But even in a highly drugged state, Michael was mumbling to himself about how he wanted to help others and how he wanted to take the money from the London concerts and build a children's hospital that would be more compassionate towards sick children. He murmured:

> Children are depressed. In those hospitals, there's no game room, no movie theater. They're sick because they're depressed. Their mind is depressing them. I want to give them that. God wants me to do it. … Don't have enough hope, no more hope. That's the next generation that's going to save our planet. … They walk around with no mother. They drop them off, they leave, a psychological degradation of that. … I feel their pain; I feel their hurt. "Heal the World," "We are the World," "Will You Be There," "The Lost Children." These are the songs I've written because I hurt.[474]

Prosecutor David Walgren stated in his closing argument:

> You hear the tragic, sad voice of Michael Jackson in some sort of drug-induced, slurred stupor, and you hear the voice of Conrad Murray, evidently seated right there, as he recorded the voice of Michael Jackson. ... For reasons unknown, it was made by Conrad Murray on his iPhone and kept on his iPhone by a doctor who will not keep a shred of medical records ... but yet on his own personal iPhone, he records Michael Jackson's voice and keeps it. Even in this state, even in this recording, with Michael at such a vulnerable state, he's talking about his plans for the future, he's talking about his desires, ... when he has no reason to believe anyone is even listening to him, when he has no reason to believe anyone will ever hear his words, when he has no reason to believe anyone would be documenting it in any way, in this vulnerable state in his own house, in his own bedroom, he is talking about what he wants to do in the future. And he is talking about his desire to build the greatest children's hospital in the world. These are his true feelings. These are his true desires. This is what he's saying in a private, vulnerable moment of what he wants to do. And for reasons unknown, for reasons completely unknown and unexplained, Conrad Murray sits by his side and records him on his iPhone.[475]

From Michael Jackson's earliest memories to his last day on earth, many who surrounded him viewed him as a money-making machine. It was impossible for him to discern whom he could trust. Murray was going to be paid, one way or another, whether through servicing Michael with propofol or through blackmail or tabloid stories.

The conflicts of interest that led to Michael's death are glaring. The concerts should never have been placed so tightly together. The rehearsal schedule should have been spread out, with plenty of rest between performances. Michael should never have been asked to decide so quickly how many concerts he would be willing to perform after demand showed he could sell out two hundred shows when he'd announced only ten. But everyone saw dollar signs, and Michael Jackson's health and well-being were lost in the process. That is not to say that no one displayed genuine concern for Michael's health, but the overall situation was rife with conflicts of interest.

Michael himself was in a vulnerable position after more than a decade of severe media slander and bullying and a grueling criminal trial in which the media dehumanized him daily. He was spoken of disparagingly by many who had never met him, including those at AEG. Shawn Trell, general counsel for AEG Live, emailed his superior, Ted Fikre, who served as general counsel for AEG (of which AEG Live was a part), to inform him he was heading to Michael's house to get him to sign the contract for the concerts. Fikre responded, "Does that mean you get to meet the freak?" Trell then replied, "Not sure how I feel about that. Interesting for sure, but kind of creepy."[476] Neither Trell nor Fikre had ever met Michael, and the company they served was set to make many millions of dollars off Michael's hard work, yet they spoke of him in the most disparaging terms. This was the sort of treatment Michael received often.

He no longer had the negotiating power he had when he was younger to dictate the terms of a performing contract. Perhaps he could have negotiated a more relaxed schedule if his image had not been so severely beaten. But a flexible schedule is costly. A nine-month rehearsal period is far more expensive than a three-month rehearsal period. Michael also very much wanted to redeem his image and perform for his fans and his children. He was tired of the stain on his name. And he died for his efforts.

After Michael's passing, the rehearsal footage was collated together and released via a documentary film in the fall of 2009. Much of the footage in the movie came from either the early rehearsals or the last two nights. Prior to the release of the documentary, and within days of Michael's passing, a short snippet was released to the press of Michael performing a portion of his song "They Don't Care About Us."

The impact of the false allegations on Michael's death should not be understated. False accusations can be very damaging to a person. In fact, various studies have shown that the falsely accused often suffer from chronic sleep disorders.[477] FACTUK, a non-profit specializing in supporting victims of unfounded allegations of abuse, wrote about the pain suffered by those who have been falsely accused:

> The experience of a wrongful allegation can quite reasonably be compared with the loss of a loved one.
>
> A bereaved person may have lost their life partner or child. The wrongfully accused may lose their reputation and sense of self-worth, their respect, and their place in their community. What's more, they can lose their career, their friends, partners, and sometimes their freedom. Also, they may have to spend their life savings on their legal defense.
>
> Whereas time may dull the pain of bereavement, the fallout from a wrongful allegation can last forever. Both the bereaved and the wrongfully accused are in dire need of support. However, while the bereaved are usually supported by their families, friends, and communities, many wrongfully accused are vilified and isolated and alone.[478]

Upon news of Michael's death, various popular websites, including the *Los Angeles Times*, Twitter, and TMZ, crashed due to the high volume of people searching for information on Michael's death. Google initially thought they were being attacked because of the high volume of searches.[479] Michael's music was played around the world as fans mourned. The concert crew was distraught. Back-up singer Judith Hill shared, "It was unfathomable. ... Everybody was in tears."[480] And, of course, no one was in more pain than

Michael's children.

Michael's nephew TJ Jackson, who became guardian to Michael's children along with their grandmother, said of his uncle:

> I truly feel that his love was too big for this world. I think simple things that he believed in—holding people, ... looking in their eyes and telling them, "I love you, I believe in you"—I think sometimes it's so sad to say, but those kinds of messages are still too pure for our world. If you're wanting to get money or do something negative, you can twist that easily and make something scandalous, but my uncle wasn't that. He was all love and beauty. ... He tried to treat everyone with such huge love and respect and tried to always give more than what people expected to make them smile.[481]

TJ's brother Taj expressed similar sentiments about their uncle:

> I feel like he was too good for this world. Especially today. I don't think a Michael Jackson can exist in today's world. It's too cynical, too selfish. You can't even do something for someone without someone saying, "Why did you do this? What do you expect from me?" It's a different world, and I always wonder, would he have survived in this world?[482]

Dr. Patrick Treacy said of Michael after his passing, "It will be a long, long time before the planet ever [again] has anybody of that level of integrity, spirituality, [and] creativity."[483]

Friend and actress Kelley Parker shared:

> We were so lucky to have had him here for the time that we did, and he accomplished what was so close to his heart—for people to love one another, to feel joy in their lives, and to believe in magic.

146

And anywhere you go in the world, when his music comes on, that is exactly what happens. People dance, sing, smile, and their spirits are lifted. What a beautiful gift he gave us.[484]

Those who had worked at Neverland also felt the pain of Michael's death. Violet Gaitan stated of her grief after Michael's passing, "It was so hard and such a deep sort of wound for me ... it was a transformation for me to understand what loss is, and what friendship is, and what love is."[485] Big Al shared how he still feels the pain of the loss, "About once a month I have a dream that I'm at Neverland and I'm getting things ready for Michael to come home and then when I wake up I'm in tears because I realize it was a dream."[486]

For Dr. Lee, Michael's death was particularly difficult because she knew his genuine desire to be healthy. She reflected on it after his passing:

> What's striking for me is he was a person who only wanted to be healthy, who only wanted the best nutrition, who only wanted the best doctor, ... and that's what tears me apart.
>
> And for a man to be so loving of other people and caring, and nobody walked in his shoes, nobody saw the pain he went through, nobody saw what he went through. I had eczema as a child. I knew what that was like; I knew how it was to be bullied.[487]

At Michael's memorial, his brother Marlon stated, through tears, "We will never understand what he endured. Not being able to walk across the street without a crowd gathering around him, being judged, ridiculed, how much pain can one take? Maybe now, Michael, they will leave you alone."[488]

14

No Resting in Peace

Can we still listen to Michael Jackson? - The Guardian

Despite his brother's pleas, there was no resting in peace for Michael Jackson. In early 2019, approaching the ten-year anniversary of Michael's passing, HBO released a slanderous documentary titled *Leaving Neverland*. The documentary interviewed two adult men who claimed that Michael Jackson molested them when they were young children in the late 1980s and early 1990s. The press reaction was brutal, with zero due diligence. The headlines ran with the assumption that these two men were telling the truth. Virtually none of the published articles investigated the veracity of the claims. For most public figures, the ten-year anniversary of their passing is a moment of remembrance and a celebration of their life. For Michael Jackson, however, the ten-year anniversary of his passing brought on the largest and most vicious attempt to "cancel" him since his 2005 child molestation trial. Countless headlines and public figures called for the censorship of his music. Oprah Winfrey posted on her Instagram account, "It's time to say goodbye to Michael Jackson." The *New York Times* ran with headlines such as, "Michael Jackson Cast a Spell. Leaving Neverland Breaks It,"[489] "The King of Pop—and Perversion,"[490] and "Reckoning with the Real Michael Jackson."[491] Countless other media outlets piled on their own insults. *Salon* posted the headline, "Letting Go of Michael Jackson: 'Leaving Neverland' Wakes Us from a False

Dream."[492] *The Guardian* asked, "Can we still listen to Michael Jackson?"[493]

What the press failed to do, however, is scrutinize the new allegations to determine their truthfulness. Once again, they did not afford Michael the basic premise of innocence until proven guilty. The press instead equated allegations with guilt. As with the previous accusations, it is essential to go back to the genesis of the new claims to understand them. The two men alleging Michael molested them are Wade Robson and James Safechuck.

Robson met Michael Jackson in 1987 when he won a dance competition sponsored by Target in Melbourne, Australia. The prize was to meet Michael Jackson. Robson was five years old at the time. The meeting was brief, only a few minutes. Robson was then invited to dance on stage at one of Michael's concerts with a group of other children. Other than on stage, he had no interaction with Michael during that performance. His mother, Joy Robson, then delivered a thank-you note to Michael's hotel room, and they got to meet Michael again, this time for approximately an hour and a half. Over the next few years, the Robsons attempted to keep in touch with Michael but never heard back from him. Then, in January and February 1990, the Robsons traveled to the United States and managed to make contact with Michael Jackson's assistant, who then arranged a meeting with Michael, who invited the family to Neverland. The Robsons returned to the United States in May 1990 when Wade was hired to participate in a commercial with Michael Jackson and other children. The Robsons ultimately immigrated to the United States so that Wade could pursue a career in the entertainment industry. They asked Michael if one of his companies would sponsor Wade to support their immigration request, and he obliged. After moving to the U.S., the Robsons rarely saw Michael. In 2005, Joy Robson testified that in the fourteen years her family had lived in the U.S. (1991–2005), they only spent four occasions at Neverland when Michael was also there. They occasionally saw Michael elsewhere, and Wade danced in several of Michael's music videos.[494] When the 1993 Jordan Chandler allegations went public, the Robsons defended Michael, and Wade denied under oath any abuse.[495]

As Robson grew up, he became a successful choreographer, creating dance routines for stars such as Britney Spears and NSYNC. During Michael's 2005 criminal child molestation trial, a former maid at Neverland who had sold stories to the tabloids in the early 1990s, instead of going to the police with her allegations, testified that she had witnessed Michael molest Wade.[496] It is worth noting that the "witnesses" who sold stories to the tabloids always claimed it was well-known children who were molested by Michael, even though many thousands of children visited Neverland, children who were not public figures. That, of course, added to the salaciousness of their stories and the sales of the tabloid magazines. Michael's defense called Wade as a defense witness, and he testified as an adult, under oath and severe cross-examination, that Michael never molested him.[497] During the trial, Robson asked Michael if he and his wife could be married at Neverland, but Michael turned down their request due to the inappropriateness of the timing.[498]

After Michael's passing in June of 2009, Robson reached out to Michael's nephew Taj Jackson to get tickets to the public memorial at the Staples Center in Los Angeles, which held approximately twenty thousand people. Robson was not invited to the private memorial. In the days and months after Michael's death, Robson had nothing but praise for Michael. He claimed Michael was "one of the main reasons I believe in the pure goodness of humankind." On June 26, 2009, just one day after Michael's passing, Wade reached out to Jeff Thacker, the co-executive producer of the hit TV show *So You Think You Can Dance*. In his email to Thacker, Robson wrote, "I wanted to write you now so if you guys are thinking of doing any dance tribute to MJ on the show, I would like it to be me who does it." Robson then participated as a dancer in a tribute by Janet Jackson to her brother at the 2009 MTV Video Music Awards in September of that year and, in October, he attended the premiere of the *This Is It* documentary, which covered the rehearsal footage for the London concerts.[499]

Not long after Michael's death, his estate teamed up with Cirque Du Soleil to create an ongoing tribute show to Michael. Cirque Du Soleil is an entertainment company that puts on circus art shows. The tribute show initially toured the world and now resides in Las Vegas. The Cirque Du Soleil entertainers perform acrobatic dances to Michael's music. On May 21, 2011, Robson sent an email to the creative team at Cirque, telling them of his interest in directing the show, "I always wanted to do this show badly. … I know that I am meant to do this show. I am passionate to do this show. I want to make it amazing for me, for you, for Cirque, and of course, Michael." In a July 2011 TV interview, Robson claimed, "I'm starting on the Cirque Du Soleil Michael Jackson show which is exciting and terrifying all at the same time because it's such a huge responsibility." The estate, however, hired someone else to direct the show. They never offered the job to Robson.[500]

During this time, Robson appeared to be in need of money. Earlier in 2011, he had auctioned off Michael Jackson memorabilia he possessed. While Robson had been a successful choreographer in his earlier years, by 2011, his career was not what it had once been. After not being hired for the Cirque Du Soleil job, Robson had few career opportunities. In late 2012, he began approaching publishers about writing a book alleging Michael Jackson had abused him, but perhaps due to the considerable advance money that Robson was seeking, no publisher picked it up.[501] On May 1, 2013, Robson filed a civil lawsuit against Michael Jackson and two of his companies, MJJ Ventures and MJJ Productions, for monetary compensation for alleged childhood sexual abuse. He also filed a creditor's claim against the Michael Jackson estate in probate court for the same.[502] The allegations went public on May 8, 2013, when Robson's lawyer declared to the tabloid TMZ that Michael was a "monster."[503] That same day, Brett Barnes, who like Robson had testified during Michael's 2005 trial that Michael had not molested him, tweeted in response to Robson's turnabout, "I wish people would realize, in your last moments on earth, all the money in the world will be of no comfort. My clear conscience will."[504]

On May 16, 2013, Robson gave an interview on the *Today* show. The following week, May 23, 2013, the Cirque Du Soleil tribute show to Michael

Jackson premiered.[505] One has to ask if Robson timed his allegations to coincide with the premier of the Cirque Du Soleil show, the show he "badly" wanted to direct but for which the entity he was now suing did not want to hire him. Did Robson make the allegations because he had few career opportunities left and felt disgruntled at the Michael Jackson estate for not hiring him? Robson wrote in a note, "My story of abuse and its effects will make me relatable/relevant. ... It's time for me to get mine!" When asked at a deposition what he meant when he said, "It's time for me to get mine!" Robson replied he did not know.[506] Would the name Wade Robson have fallen into oblivion without the allegations? Brandi Jackson, Michael Jackson's niece, dated Robson as a teenager. She proclaimed, "He has always been a bit of an opportunist. ... He gets this from his mother. He knows how to position himself into different situations that will benefit him in a financial way. So, once he had nothing else to climb for, once he was being taken off of the Cirque Du Soleil show, and other jobs weren't coming through, this was his next outlet."[507] Indeed, on the surface, Robson's actions may seem inconsistent, in the sense that he went from praising Michael to accusing him of molestation, but when viewed through the lens of an opportunist, they were quite consistent. Less than twenty-four hours after Michael's death, Robson was offering himself to partake in tribute events, capitalizing on Michael's passing. Once Robson's career had dried up, he appears to have found other ways to capitalize on his connection to Michael.

So, how did Robson explain his 180-degree turn? He attempted to clarify his sudden metamorphosis in various inconsistent and contradictory ways. In the *Leaving Neverland* documentary, Robson claimed he was in love with Michael. Other explanations he has offered were: he did not know it was abuse, he thought he would go to jail, he was taught to lie about abuse, he did not want Michael to go to prison, he felt shame, and Michael Jackson's lawyers bullied him.[508] If he did not know it was abuse, why would he worry that he or Michael might go to prison for it and why would he feel shame? Is it realistic to believe that a grown man who testifies in a criminal trial does not understand what abuse is?

And contrary to the allegations of Jordan Chandler and Gavin Arvizo, Robson claimed Jackson regularly anally raped him.[509] Robson's allegations were far more brutal than either Chandler's or Arvizo's. Chandler and Arvizo were young when they made their allegations, and rape could have been easily verified via a medical exam. Robson was an adult when he made his allegations; hence, he could be far bolder with his claims. And the media loved it. With each Michael Jackson allegation, the alleged crimes became more horrific. But Robson claimed he was abused in the early 1990s, before Chandler. So even though his accusations came after Chandler's and Arvizo's, the alleged molestation occurred earlier. Typically, an abuser becomes more aggressive with time, not less. So, Robson's claims of the brutality of the molestation do not correlate with the timeline. His allegations of constant rape also do not correlate with the known facts. In the alleged seven-year abuse period, Michael Jackson was only at Neverland Ranch once at the same time as Robson was.[510] One must also ask, why would Michael Jackson agree to have Wade Robson testify at his 2005 trial if he had abused him? Robson was called as a defense witness, not a prosecution witness. And Jackson's defense attorney was already calling Macaulay Culkin and Brett Barnes to the stand, so Robson's testimony did not add all that much to Michael's defense. In retrospect, the photos of Robson arriving at and leaving the 2005 trial are indicative of his opportunist persona. Both Culkin and Barnes were quiet and professional when arriving and leaving the courthouse. On the other hand, Robson was smiling and giving peace signs to the press, hamming it up for the cameras.

Why did Robson claim he did not know it was abuse? Because he needed to, in order to meet the statute of limitations in filing claims for compensation. If he had known all along that he was abused he would have been outside of the statute of limitations for seeking compensation. Robson filed two separate legal actions against Jackson's entities, both seeking monetary payout: One was a creditor's claim against Michael's estate in probate court and the other was a lawsuit against Jackson and two of his companies, MJJ Productions and MJJ Ventures.

To file a creditor's claim against a deceased's estate, one must do so within sixty days of having knowledge of the administration of the estate. Here, Robson's claims are provably false, as he sought employment from the estate, so he was clearly aware of their existence long before he filed his creditor's claim. He declared, under penalty of perjury, that he did not know of the administration of the estate prior to March 4, 2013. However, Robson visited with John Branca, the executor of the Michael Jackson Estate, in 2011, seeking the Cirque Du Soleil job. The court dismissed Robson's creditor's claim on May 26, 2015, the judge declaring that no reasonable person could believe Robson's claims that he did not know the estate existed.[511]

That left Robson with only the civil lawsuit against Jackson's companies. In his civil suit, Robson claimed that the two Jackson companies served as "the most sophisticated public child sexual abuse procurement and facilitation organization the world has known." However, it was not Michael's companies who sponsored the dance competition that Robson won at age five that allowed him to meet Michael. Target, Pepsi, and CBS Records organized and sponsored the event. When the Robsons moved to the United States, it was Wade's mother, Joy, who asked Michael if his company would sponsor them, to which he agreed. Joy Robson testified to this under oath. This was a one-off favor, not something Jackson's companies typically did. And it was the Robsons that sought out Michael, not the other way around.[512] This hardly makes the two companies "the most sophisticated public child sexual abuse procurement and facilitation organization the world has known." As of the publication date of this book, Robson's lawsuit is still in the court system. No doubt the *Leaving Neverland* documentary was a way of putting pressure on and prejudicing a potential jury.

How did the second accuser, James Safechuck, come into the picture? Safechuck met Michael in the 1980s when he was cast to appear in a commercial with him. Safechuck's family business, Sea/Sue Inc., was sued for $800,000 on April 26, 2013, just a few weeks before Robson's allegations went public.[513] Safechuck told Oprah Winfrey that it was only when he saw

Robson on television, in May of 2013, that he realized that he too had been molested by Michael Jackson. Or is it more likely that Safechuck realized that joining Robson in suing Michael could easily and quickly solve his financial troubles? Shortly after seeing Robson make his allegations on TV, Safechuck filed a lawsuit for monetary compensation for the alleged molestation. As of the publication date of this book, his suit also is still pending in the courts.

Safechuck's allegations suffer from massive credibility issues. The most glaringly false tale Safechuck told in the *Leaving Neverland* documentary was his claim that Michael molested him at the Neverland train station. In the documentary, Safechuck recounted in detail how Jackson allegedly molested him "every day" at the train station during the "honeymoon phase" of their relationship in the late 1980s. It is often said of abuse allegations that no one will ever know the truth other than the two people who were in the room. However, we know the truth in this case because the room did not exist. Permits granted by Santa Barbara County prove that the local authorities did not approve the construction of the train station until September 1993. The building was not completed until mid-1994. Many photographs support the dates stated in the permits. Thus, the train station was not built until years after the alleged abuse occurred. Even if Safechuck is given leniency about his claims that the alleged abuse happened during the "honeymoon phase," and we assume it happened later in the abuse period, Safechuck declared, under penalty of perjury, that the abuse stopped in 1992 as he was becoming too old for Michael Jackson. Indeed, the entire premise of the documentary is that Jackson dumps boys as they reach puberty. By the time Safechuck could have been feasibly abused by Michael Jackson in the train station, he would have been bigger than Jackson, and it would have been two years after the abuse stopped, according to the dates Safechuck gave under penalty of perjury. Therefore, one glaring error renders the entire case a sham: Safechuck claimed he was abused by Jackson regularly at the train station in the late 1980s and that all abuse by Jackson stopped in 1992 because Safechuck had become too old for Jackson, but the train station did not exist until 1994.[514]

There are other massive credibility issues with Safechuck's allegations. Like Robson, he has told different stories about when he realized he had been abused. He told Oprah that he realized it when he saw Robson on TV in May 2013. In a sworn declaration, Safechuck claimed he told his mother in 2005, albeit in an indirect way, about the molestation. He told her that Michael was a "bad man" and that "something had happened." Later, in the same sworn declaration, he claimed he needed psychiatric help when he saw Robson on TV in 2013. He claimed it was through the "help of a therapist" that he was "finally able to begin to recognize that he was a victim of childhood sexual abuse." Did he realize he was abused when he saw Robson on TV or when he went to a therapist? And how could he have told his mother about it in 2005 if he did not realize it until 2013?[515]

In *Leaving Neverland*, his mother shared her reaction when Michael died, "I was so happy he died. Thank God he can't hurt any more children." Michael died in 2009, before the 2013 date that Safechuck gave in his sworn declaration and his interview with Oprah as being the date he realized Michael had abused him. She claims to have celebrated Michael's death and assumed he had hurt children based on her alleged brief conversation with her son in 2005 that Michael was a "bad man."[516]

Another ludicrous claim made by Safechuck is that Jackson called him and begged him to testify for him at his 2005 criminal trial. Safechuck claimed, "I said no, and he got really angry at me. He threatened me with his lawyers and said that I had perjured myself years ago. And that he has the best lawyers in the world and that they were going to get me." There are two massive issues with this claim. The first is that Michael did not put on a character defense during his 2005 trial. There was not a single character witness called. The only reason Robson was called to testify is because another individual had sold stories to the tabloids claiming she had seen Robson molested by Michael. Robson was only asked to testify to dispute her testimony and for no other reason. No one testified at the trial about seeing Safechuck molested; hence, there was no reason to call him to testify for Michael. The second issue with Safechuck's claim is the notion that Jackson would go after him for committing perjury in the early 1990s when Safechuck swore he had not been molested by Michael. If Michael went after Safechuck for perjury, then he would be admitting that he molested him. Furthermore, if Safechuck did not realize he was abused until 2013, then why would he have been hesitant to testify for Michael or scared that Michael would come after him for perjury? Jackson's 2005 lawyer, Tom Mesereau, confirmed that the defense never considered calling Safechuck to testify.[517]

Yet another discrepancy in Safechuck's allegations is that he claimed to have been molested for the first time in the summer of 1988, during the Paris leg of Michael's *Bad* tour.[518] Safechuck then declared that he was molested in early 1989 when Michael performed at the Grammy Awards. However, Michael did not perform at the Grammy Awards in 1989. He performed at the awards show in 1988, which was prior to the first time that Safechuck had alleged he was molested. It is not impossible for Safechuck to get his years wrong, but it is questionable that he claims the molestation at the Grammys occurred after the first time he was molested; however, the Grammys happened prior to the first time he was allegedly molested.[519]

There are numerous other discrepancies in Robson's and Safechuck's claims—far too many to list. Beyond their graphic details of alleged molestation, Robson and Safechuck had nothing to offer to support their claims other than a few notes Michael had written to them. However, many children who had worked with or spent time with Michael have similar messages and letters that they received from him.[520]

For decades, the corporate media has treated the molestation allegations leveled against Michael as if they were facts. It has relied on salacious accusations and graphic details of alleged molestation rather than evidence. But each accusation, starting with the Chandler allegations, suffers from massive credibility issues. Each falls apart under scrutiny. Furthermore, by the media unquestioningly accepting each allegation, it only encourages others who are disgruntled or in financial need to also make false claims. Journalist John Zieglar argued, "If Wade Robson and James Safechuck are believed ... then anybody will be believed, no matter how ridiculous the claim. These claims are the most easily discredited in a logical world that I've seen in my life."[521]

The press will argue, "Where there's smoke, there's fire." There have been four allegations made against Michael (Chandler, Arvizo, Robson, and Safechuck); hence, they must be true. But that is not how it works. Each must be analyzed independently, and if none stands up under scrutiny, then the volume of allegations cannot be used as evidence of guilt. Furthermore, the average pedophile has 240 victims over the course of a lifetime, far more than the four who have accused Michael.[522] All four went to civil attorneys seeking compensation. There has never been a single accuser who simply went to the police, told a consistent story, and reported the alleged crime. Moreover, all four were very publicly seen with Jackson, either in his music videos, in commercials, at awards shows, or in a documentary. If Michael were to have abused children, would he not have chosen children that he was not so publicly linked to? Jesus Salas, the house manager at Neverland for approximately twenty years, testified in court that he had seen hundreds of thousands of children visit the Neverland property, each having a wonderful time.[523]

The *Leaving Neverland* "documentary" should have been shunned and mocked. And indeed, it was by many. Numerous viewers posted comments online that the film was nothing more than "bad acting." The press, however, cried out for the cancellation of Michael's music. It was not enough that they tormented Michael in life; they tried to destroy his memory and his music in death. There was no resting in peace for Michael Jackson.

15

Conclusion

The rarest courage of all—for the skill to pursue it is given to very few men—is the courage to wage a silent battle to illuminate the nature of man and the world in which he lives. - John F. Kennedy

The story of Michael Jackson can teach us much about our society. It is a story about how power works, how media works, and how we as a people respond to what we are told.

It is often claimed that Michael Jackson was trashed for profit. After all, negative gossip sells. However, do such conclusions tell us the whole story? The 2019 slanderous "documentary" *Leaving Neverland* was HBO's third-highest-rated documentary in a decade but still only received 1.29 million viewers on the night it aired, despite weeks of heavy promotion by many corporate media outlets.[524] By comparison, when HBO aired Michael Jackson's Bucharest concert in 1992, 3.7 million homes viewed it.[525] When Oprah aired her interview with Michael Jackson in early 1993, before the allegations, 90 million people watched it.[526] These numbers show that interest in Michael Jackson was far greater than the interest in those trashing him. Why, then, did the press mercilessly attack him? Why did they rarely disclose the multitude of issues that surrounded the molestation claims? Why did they not better explain the timeline of events that led to each allegation?

159

Groupthink in the press is very powerful; few reporters will diverge from mainstream narratives on any topic. Those who stray risk not staying employed. The mainstream corporate media is a tool of empire. They spread propaganda and mold our society. They convince us that war is worth fighting. They shape our culture. And they dehumanize their enemies.

Michael Jackson brought light and love to the world. His music touched people's hearts profoundly—across cultures, languages, and geographic regions. It was not uncommon for fans to shed tears of strong emotion as they watched him perform. Music is a potent form of communication. Politicians can speak, and the media can propagandize, but artists can touch people at their core. Michael's music displayed empathy, compassion, kindness, and courage. President John F. Kennedy once said of courage when speaking about poetry, "There are many kinds of courage: bravery under fire, the courage to risk reputation and friendship and career for convictions which are deeply held, but perhaps the rarest courage of all—for the skill to pursue it is given to very few men—is the courage to wage a silent battle to illuminate the nature of man and the world in which he lives."[527] Michael tried to reach into the goodness that resides in most of humanity and bring it to the forefront. But do those who deploy divide-and-conquer tactics want a unified society? Today, much of the entertainment industry is shallow and superficial. Most artists promote mainstream narratives; they do not speak out against them. They do not question the wars that are fought or the culture that is pushed. But JFK proclaimed that art should not be a form of propaganda but a form of truth. He expressed, "The highest duty of the writer, the composer, the artist is to remain true to himself and let the chips fall where they may."[528] There is no doubt Michael remained authentic in his art and paid dearly for it.

It is not surprising that Michael Jackson was so viciously attacked. Darkness always seeks to extinguish light. Evil always wants to destroy good. The Western media obsessed daily over the Michael Jackson allegations as they obscured the many war crimes being committed. Michael was not unaware of the disdain that some in positions of power held for him. His son Prince revealed, "He would come home worried about his safety, about his career, about his assets, because he felt that he was pissing off the wrong people and it was putting a target on his back either through his messages of unity or calling out other entities, for whatever reason it was, it was putting a target on his back."[529] Michael's vocal director, Kevin Dorsey, said Michael had confided to him, "You know I'm not going to live long. Look at history. ... They don't want me to live long. I bring too much love. I bring too much peace and happiness and joy to the world, to all people, to every race, every religion, to every culture. They don't want that. They don't want that."[530]

Despite Michael's awareness of the nefarious interests he was up against, he continued to share his talent and hope for humanity with the world. Regarding Michael's outlook, studio engineer Matt Forger stated, "He viewed the world and humanity as having so much potential. I know he was frustrated personally with the feeling that things should be so much better than they are on the earth for everyone and all of the life that is on the earth."[531] Despite all the attacks, Michael never lost his faith in God, nor his love for children, who he believed were a reflection of God. Michael's music was inspired by creation, and he revealed how children playing sparked him to write the song "Speechless": "[Children] are so innocent. They are the quintessential form of innocence. Just being in their presence, I felt completely speechless because I felt I was looking in the face of God."[532] Michael often said in interviews that Jesus said to be like children, to be as pure as children.

It was not easy being Michael Jackson, however. Many could not understand his childlike qualities. The media demonized them as something sinister and evil. He dealt with more pressure, public scrutiny, and bullying than arguably any human being could withstand. But despite all the struggles and the slander, Michael carried forward. In his song "Will You Be There," Michael reflected on how one must always press on, no matter the obstacles, but admitted, "I'm only human." There is no denying that he suffered much pain over the false allegations.

In the 1990s, he wrote "The Innocent Man." In the lyrics, he shared the isolation he felt and how his faith in God carried him through it. He feared he would die a man without a country, rejected by all, but he could accept the exile as long as God knew he was innocent.

Michael Jackson's story reveals a lot about our culture. It shows us how we too easily trust the media and too readily take allegations at face value instead of digging deeper to look for the truth. It puts on display how ugly we as a society can act toward someone pure and innocent. We celebrate artists who sing one superficial song after another and demonized the artist who tried to unite us and who brought to light our shared humanity.

As Malcolm X warned:

> The media is the most powerful entity on earth. They have the power to make the innocent guilty and the guilty innocent, and that's power because they control the minds of the masses. The press is so powerful … it can make the criminal look like he's the victim, and make the victim look like he's the criminal. … If you're not careful, the newspapers will have you hating the people who are being oppressed and loving the people who are doing the oppressing.

But not everyone fell for the defamatory treatment of Michael, and the fog continues to lift for others. Michael's son Prince spoke of how many fans share their love for his father with him, "He was such an incredible person, and the message and the music and everything about that is still just as much cherished, if not more, today, and because of his legacy, for some reason, it translates down to me. And I don't know how to explain it. It's just overwhelming love."[533]

Michael put his heart and soul into his art. He once shared, "Like Michaelangelo said, 'I know the creator will go, but his work survives, that is why to escape death, I attempt to bind my soul to my work,' and that's how I feel."[534] Michael believed strongly that music was eternal. He proclaimed, "Great music and great melodies are immortal. ... Fashions change, culture changes, customs change. Great music is immortal. We still listen to Mozart today ... any of the greats. ... It's forever, for generations upon generations to appreciate, forever. ... I know that's a fact."[535]

Michael once stated that he wanted his music to be "a voice for the voiceless."[536] There is no reason it cannot be. In defiance of the decades of slander, Michael Jackson's music lives on. His songs resonate as much today as they did when he first wrote and recorded them—from "They Don't Care About Us" to "Heal the World" to "Man in the Mirror" and countless others. It is a testament to how his music touched people that it survived the endless attempts to destroy the man and his legacy. Despite its best efforts, darkness can never extinguish light.

Notes

PREFACE

1   Remarks at a Closed-Circuit Television Broadcast on Behalf of the National Cultural Center, November 29, 1962, John F. Kennedy Presidential Library and Museum, https://www.jfklibrary.org/asset-viewer/archives/JFKWHA/1962/JFKWHA-145-008/JFKWHA-145-008.

2   Michael Jackson interview, *Oprah*, 1993, https://www.youtube.com/watch?v=NvR60pAg0JI.

A STAR IS BORN

3   Mike Smallcombe, *Making Michael* (New York, NY: Clink Street Publishing, 2016), 13.

4   Katherine Jackson testimony, Katherine Jackson v. AEG, https://www.teammichaeljackson.com/jackson-v-aeg-the-trial/.

5   Michael Jackson, *Moon Walk* (New York, NY: Harmony Books, 2009), 6.

6   Michael Jackson interview, *Geraldo Rivera*, 2005, https://www.youtube.com/watch?v=7u-Hl_K5nqQ.

7   Michael Jackson interview, *Keep Hope Alive with Jesse Jackson*, 2005, https://www.youtube.com/watch?v=s6kg2CCschI.

8   Michael Jackson interview, *Geraldo Rivera*, 2005, https://www.youtube.com/watch?v=7u-Hl_K5nqQ.

9   Jackson, *Moon Walk*, 29.

10   Ibid., 33.

11   Ibid., 36–37.

12   Ibid., 38–39.

13   Ibid., 43.

14   Ibid., 45–47.

15   Ibid., 50.

16   Ibid., 50–67.

17   Michael Jackson memorial service, July 7, 2009, https://www.youtube.com/watch?v=3vibRwe8iCk.

18   Katherine Jackson testimony, Katherine Jackson v. AEG, https://www.teammichaeljacks on.com/jackson-v-aeg-the-trial/.

19   Michael Jackson memorial service, July 7, 2009, https://www.youtube.com/watch?v=3vi bRwe8iCk.

20   Michael Jackson interview, *Oprah*, 1993, https://www.youtube.com/watch?v=NvR6OpAg 0JI.

21   Jackson, *Moon Walk*, 68.

22   Michael Jackson interview, *Keep Hope Alive with Jesse Jackson*, 2005, https://www.youtube. com/watch?v=s6kg2CCschI.

23   Jackson, *Moon Walk*, 78.

24   Michael Jackson interview, *Ebony/Jet*, 1987, https://www.youtube.com/watch?v=9hARx BrSsa8.

25   Michael Jackson interview, *Oprah*, 1993, https://www.youtube.com/watch?v=NvR6OpAg 0JI.

26   Oxford University speech, 2001, https://www.youtube.com/watch?v=PkElyPTY1u8.

27   Michael Jackson interview, *Geraldo Rivera*, 2005, https://www.youtube.com/watch?v=7u-HL_K5nqQ.

28   Jackson, *Moon Walk*, 95–96.

29   David Nordahl interview, *Reflections on The Dance*, http://www.reflectionsonthedance.co m/interviewwithdavidnordahl.html.

30   Jackson, *Moon Walk*, 97.

31   Ibid., 114–115.

32   Ibid., 122.

33   Tim McPhate, "Michael Jackson 'Thriller' Reaches Billboard Chart Milestone," Recording Academy Grammy Awards, https://www.grammy.com/news/michael-jackson-thriller-re aches-billboard-chart-milestone.

UNEXPECTED CHALLENGES

34   Jackson, *Moon Walk*, 235–237.

35   Debbie Rowe testimony, Katherine Jackson v. AEG, https://www.teammichaeljackson.co m/jackson-v-aeg-the-trial/.

36   Carol LaMere interview, *MJ Cast*, Episode 133, June 12, 2021, https://www.themjcast.co m/133-vindication-day-special-with-carol-lamere/.

37   About Vitiligo, VR Foundation, https://vrfoundation.org/about_vitiligo.

38   Smallcombe, *Making Michael*, 83.

39   Kerry Ludlam, "Lupus Photosensitivity and UV Light," WebMD, https://www.webmd.co m/lupus/lupus-photosensitivity-uv#:~:text=Many%20experience%20an%20increase%20i n,and%20cheeks%20after%20sun%20exposure.

40   Debbie Rowe testimony, Katherine Jackson v. AEG, https://www.teammichaeljackson.co
      m/jackson-v-aeg-the-trial/.

41   Carol LaMere interview, *MJ Cast*, Episode 133, June 12, 2021, https://www.themjcast.co
      m/133-vindication-day-special-with-carol-lamere/.

42   David Nordahl interview, *Reflections on the Dance*, http://www.reflectionsonthedance.co
      m/interviewwithdavidnordahl.html.

43   Matt Forger interview, *MJ Cast*, Episode 151, December 30, 2022, https://www.themjcast.
      com/151-matt-forger-special-part-2/.

44   David Nordahl interview, *Reflections on the Dance*, http://www.reflectionsonthedance.co
      m/interviewwithdavidnordahl.html.

45   John E. Harris, "Did Michael Jackson Have Vitiligo?" January 18, 2016, UMass CHAN
      Medical School, https://www.umassmed.edu/vitiligo/blog/blog-posts1/2016/01/did-mi
      chael-jackson-have-vitiligo/#:~:text=and%20use%20Benoquin.-,Did%20Michael%20Jack
      son%20have%20vitiligo%3F,diagnosis%20in%20his%20medical%20history.

46   David Nordahl interview, *Reflections on the Dance*, http://www.reflectionsonthedance.co
      m/interviewwithdavidnordahl.html.

47   Michael Jackson interview, *Oprah*, 1993, https://www.youtube.com/watch?v=NvR60pAg
      0JI.

48   Dr. Patrick Treacy interview, December 3, 2011, https://www.youtube.com/watch?v=O
      G_kClc0Jho.

49   *Square One*, directed by Danny Wu (Danny Wu, 2019), streaming video.

50   Smallcombe, *Making Michael*, 85.

51   Ibid., 87–91.

52   "'We Are the World' Released as a Single," Michael Jackson Official Website, https://www.
      michaeljackson.com/news/we-are-world-released-single/.

53   Ben Sisario, "Sony to pay Michael Jackson Estate $750 million for stake in music
      catalog," *New York Times*, nytimes.com/2016/03/15/business/media/sony-to-pay-michael-
      jacksons-estate-750-million-for-stake-in-music-catalog.html.

54   Smallcombe, *Making Michael*, 100.

55   Joseph Vogel, "How Michael Jackson Made 'Bad,'" *The Atlantic*, September 10, 2012,
      https://www.theatlantic.com/entertainment/archive/2012/09/how-michael-jackso
      n-made-bad/262162/.

56   Michael Jackson's private tape recordings with Shmuley Boteach, 2000–2001, https://ww
      w.youtube.com/watch?v=sYC87HPNWA0.

57   Guiseppe Mazzola, "Michael Jackson: Take 2 (The Footage You Were Never Meant to
      See)," February 23, 2003, https://www.youtube.com/watch?v=utW8SlB5ZFw.

58   Ibid.

59 Ibid.

60 Michael Jackson private home movies, 2003, https://www.youtube.com/watch?v=BLji_UBM6Kw&t.

61 Michael Jackson interview, *Get Music*, 2001, https://www.youtube.com/watch?v=heCJbos7dfE.

62 Michael Jackson interview, *Barbra Walters*, September 7, 1997, https://www.youtube.com/watch?v=gFIjGn4yA6c.

63 Michael Jackson interview, *Ebony/Jet*, 1987, https://www.youtube.com/watch?v=9hARxBrSsa8.

64 Handwritten note published in *People*, October 12, 1987, https://www.michaeljacksonslegacy.org/michael/michael-jackson-in-his-own-words/.

MICHAEL, THE MAN

65 Michael Jackson's private tape recordings with Shmuley Boteach, 2000–2001, https://www.youtube.com/watch?v=sYC87HPNWA0.

66 Ibid.

67 Smallcombe, *Making Michael*, 163.

68 David Nordahl interview, *Reflections on the Dance*, http://www.reflectionsonthedance.com/interviewwithdavidnordahl.html.

69 Ibid.

70 Ibid.

71 Ibid.

72 David Nordahl follow-up interview, *Reflections on the Dance*, 2013, https://www.youtube.com/watch?v=o1ueCdlSOlo.

73 Brad Sundberg interview, *The Hustle*, March 16, 2019, https://thehustle.podbean.com/e/bonus-brad-sundberg-technical-director-for-michael-jackson/.

74 TJ Jackson interview, *MJ Cast*, Episode 126, December 18, 2020, https://www.themjcast.com/126-tj-jackson-special/.

75 Allan Scanlan interview, *Happy Michael Jackson Day*, https://www.youtube.com/watch?v=4viLuS9un0Q.

76 Michael Jackson interview, *Ebony/Jet*, 1987, https://www.youtube.com/watch?v=9hARxBrSsa8.

77 Brad Sundberg interview, *MJ Cast*, Episode 15, August 29, 2015, https://www.themjcast.com/episode-015-brad-sundberg-special/.

78 Violet Gaitan interview, *MJ Cast*, Episode 149, November 6, 2022, https://www.themjcast.com/149-violet-gaitan-booker-special/.

79 Harrison Funk interview, *MJ Cast*, Episode 94, January 14, 2019, https://www.themjcast.com/episode-094-harrison-funk-special/.

80   Brad Buxer interview, *MJ Cast*, Episode 100, May 5, 2019, https://www.themjcast.com/episode-100-brad-buxer-special/.

81   Rory Kaplan interview, *Red Jackson Dance*, October 15, 2022, https://www.youtube.com/watch?v=6IbFIoTcd14&t=2862s.

82   Kevin Dorsey interview, *MJ Cast*, Episode 115, March 15, 2020, https://www.themjcast.com/episode-115-kevin-dorsey-special/.

83   Miko Brando interview, *ABC News*, July 16, 2009, https://www.youtube.com/watch?v=-k3x-8nt8IY.

84   Smallcombe, *Making Michael*, 166.

85   Steven Paul Whitsitt interview, *MJ Cast*, Episode 118, May 26, 2020, https://www.themjcast.com/118-steven-paul-whitsitt-special/.

86   Rob Hoffman interview, *MJ Cast*, Episode 30, May 6, 2016, https://www.themjcast.com/episode-030-rob-hoffman-special/.

87   Vincent Paterson interview, *MJ Cast*, Episode 64, August 28, 2017, https://www.themjcast.com/episode-064-vincent-paterson-special/.

88   Dick Zimmerman interview, *MJ Cast*, Episode 86, August 17, 2018, https://www.themjcast.com/episode-086-dick-zimmerman-special/.

89   Brad Sundberg interview, *The Hustle*, March 16, 2019, https://thehustle.podbean.com/e/bonus-brad-sundberg-technical-director-for-michael-jackson/.

90   Jimmy Van Norman interview, *Red Jackson Dance*, September 23, 2023, https://www.youtube.com/watch?v=iVURfHs2W3I&t=1797s.

91   Eddie Garcia interview, *MJ Cast*, Episode 122, August 29, 2020, https://www.themjcast.com/122-eddie-garcia-special/.

92   Carol LaMere interview, *MJ Cast*, Episode 133, June 12, 2021, https://www.themjcast.com/133-vindication-day-special-with-carol-lamere/.

93   Michael Jackson interview, *Geraldo Rivera*, 2005, https://www.youtube.com/watch?v=7u-Hl_K5nqQ.

A BETTER WORLD

94   Smallcombe, *Making Michael*, 123.

95   Charles Thomson interview, *MJ Cast*, Episode 98, March 31, 2019, https://www.themjcast.com/episode-098-we-had-a-breakallegedly/.

96   Jackson, *Moon Walk*, 265–268.

97   Michael Jackson interview, *Ebony/Jet*, 1987, https://www.youtube.com/watch?v=9hARxBrSsa8.

NEVERLAND

98   Smallcombe, *Making Michael*, 126.

99 Ibid., 130.

100 David Nordahl interview, *Reflections on the Dance.*

101 Smallcombe, *Making Michael*, 130.

102 Allan Scanlan interview, *MJ Cast*, Episode 107, August 24, 2019, https://www.themjcast.com/episode-107-allan-big-al-scanlan-special/.

103 Ibid.

104 Violet Gaitan interview, *MJ Cast*, Episode 149, November 6, 2022, https://www.themjcast.com/149-violet-gaitan-booker-special/.

105 Allan Scanlan interview, *MJ Book Club*, October 31, 2020, https://www.youtube.com/watch?v=SHmEPM7Yy9s&t.

106 Allan Scanlan interview, *MJ Cast*, Episode 107, August 24, 2019, https://www.themjcast.com/episode-107-allan-big-al-scanlan-special/.

107 David Nordahl interview, *Reflections on the Dance.*

108 Michael Jackson interview, *Geraldo Rivera*, 2005, https://www.youtube.com/watch?v=7u-Hl_K5nqQ.

109 Smallcombe, *Making Michael*, 269.

110 Allan Scanlan interview, *MJ Cast*, Episode 107, August 24, 2019, https://www.themjcast.com/episode-107-allan-big-al-scanlan-special/.

111 Brad Buxer interview, *MJ Cast*, Episode 100, May 5, 2019, https://www.themjcast.com/episode-100-brad-buxer-special/.

112 Michael Jackson interview with Steve Harvey, https://www.youtube.com/watch?v=RW5poJgHXU4.

113 Allan Scanlan interview, *MJ Cast*, Episode 107, August 24, 2019, https://www.themjcast.com/episode-107-allan-big-al-scanlan-special/.

114 Ibid., and Violet Gaitan interview, *MJ Cast*, Episode 149, November 6, 2022, https://www.themjcast.com/149-violet-gaitan-booker-special/ and Allan Scanlan interview, *Humanitarian—The Real Michael Jackson*, August 24, 2023, https://www.humanitarianmj.com/ neverlands-purpose-with-allan-big-al-scanlan/.

115 Michael Jackson interview, *Oprah*, 1993, https://www.youtube.com/watch?v=NvR60pAg0JI.

116 Allan Scanlan interview, *MJ Cast*, Episode 107, August 24, 2019, https://www.themjcast.com/episode-107-allan-big-al-scanlan-special/.

117 David Nordahl interview, *Reflections on the Dance.*

118 Allan Scanlan interview, *Humanitarian—The Real Michael Jackson*, August 24, 2023, https://www.humanitarianmj.com/neverlands-purpose-with-allan-big-al-scanlan/.

119 Violet Gaitan interview, *MJ Cast*, Episode 149, November 6, 2022, https://www.themjcast.com/149-violet-gaitan-booker-special/.

120 Allan Scanlan interview, *MJ Cast*, Episode 107, August 24, 2019, https://www.themjcast.com/episode-107-allan-big-al-scanlan-special/.

121 Ibid.

122 Allan Scanlan interview, *Happy Michael Jackson Day*, https://www.youtube.com/watch?v=4viLuS9un0Q.

123 Ibid.

124 Michael Jackson interview, *60 Minutes*, December 25, 2003, https://www.youtube.com/watch?v=-GF2JUe-2Is.

125 Allan Scanlan interview, *MJ Cast*, Episode 107, August 24, 2019, https://www.themjcast.com/episode-107-allan-big-al-scanlan-special/.

126 Michael Jackson interview, *Geraldo Rivera*, 2005, https://www.youtube.com/watch?v=7u-Hl_K5nqQ.

127 David Nordahl interview, *Reflections on the Dance*.

128 Mazzola, "Michael Jackson: Take 2."

129 David Nordahl follow-up interview, *Reflections on the Dance*, 2013.

130 Allan Scanlan interview, *MJ Book Club*, October 31, 2020, https://www.youtube.com/watch?v=SHmEPM7Yy9s&t.

131 Allan Scanlan interview, *Happy Michael Jackson Day*, https://www.youtube.com/watch?v=4viLuS9un0Q.

132 Allan Scanlan interview, *MJ Cast*, Episode 107, August 24, 2019, https://www.themjcast.com/episode-107-allan-big-al-scanlan-special/.

133 Violet Gaitan interview, *MJ Cast*, Episode 149, November 6, 2022, https://www.themjcast.com/149-violet-gaitan-booker-special/.

134 Allan Scanlan interview, *Happy Michael Jackson Day*, https://www.youtube.com/watch?v=4viLuS9un0Q.

135 Allan Scanlan interview, *MJ Book Club*, October 31, 2020, https://www.youtube.com/watch?v=SHmEPM7Yy9s&t.

136 Ibid.

137 Allan Scanlan interview, *Happy Michael Jackson Day*, https://www.youtube.com/watch?v=4viLuS9un0Q.

138 Ibid. and Talitha Linehan interview, *MJ Cast*, episode 129, April 4, 2021, https://www.youtube.com/watch?v=JF29GLifal0.

139 Jackson, Jermaine, *You Are Not Alone* (New York, NY: Touchstone, 2011), 8.

140 Gwen Carino interview, *Humanitarian—The Real Michael Jackson*, August 10, 2023, https://www.humanitarianmj.com/michael-jackson-at-the-orphans-christmas-party-with-gwen-carino/.

141 2006 World Music Awards, Beyoncé Knowles introduction, https://www.youtube.com/watch?v=WviiygVo3Oc.

142 David Nordahl follow-up interview, *Reflections on the Dance*, 2013.

143 Patrick Treacy interview, September 26, 2010, https://www.youtube.com/watch?v=OMW7PXqU2Vg.

144 Jennifer Love Hewitt interview, *Jimmy Kimmel Live*, uploaded September 5, 2018, https://www.youtube.com/watch?v=UCWnQ0vE5d4.

145 Carol LaMere interview, *MJ Cast*, Episode 133, June 12, 2021, https://www.themjcast.com/133-vindication-day-special-with-carol-lamere/.

146 Taj Jackson interview, *MJ Cast*, episode 20, November 15, 2015, https://www.themjcast.com/episode-020-taj-jackson-special/.

147 Prince Jackson interview, *Good Morning Britain*, October 28, 2021, https://www.youtube.com/watch?v=weStmn5qmyw.

MICHAEL'S VOICE

148 Smallcombe, *Making Michael*, 6.

149 Joseph Vogel, "Black and White: How *Dangerous* Kicked Off Michael Jackson's Race Paradox," *The Guardian*, March 17, 2018, https://www.theguardian.com/music/2018/mar/17/black-and-white-how-dangerous-kicked-off-michael-jacksons-race-paradox.

150 Glenn Plaskin, "Out of the Mouth of Michael ...," *Chicago Tribune*, August 16, 1992, https://www.chicagotribune.com/news/ct-xpm-1992-08-16-9203140099-story.html.

151 Joshua Bloom and Waldo E. Martin Jr., *Black Against Empire* (Berkeley, CA: University of California Press, 2013), 2.

152 Ibid., 10.

153 Michael Jackson interview, *Get Music*, 2001, https://www.youtube.com/watch?v=heCJbos7dfE.

154 Michael Jackson, handwritten song lyrics, https://michaeljacksonnotes.wordpress.com/2014/07/15/palestine-dont-cry/.

155 Michael Jackson interview, *Keep Hope Alive with Jesse Jackson*, 2005, https://www.youtube.com/watch?v=s6kg2CCschI.

156 Matt Forger interview, *MJ Cast*, Episode 151, December 30, 2022, https://www.themjcast.com/151-matt-forger-special-part-2/.

THE MUSIC AND THE DANCE

157 Michael Jackson speech, 1993 Grammy Awards, https://www.youtube.com/watch?v=Vt4aH3dypio.

158 *Living with Michael Jackson*, directed by Julie Shaw (Granada Television, 2003), TV documentary, https://www.youtube.com/watch?v=bfAyV_4dULk&list=PL33366168B76D3205&index=3.

159 Jimmy Van Norman interview, *Red Jackson Dance*, September 23, 2023, https://www.yout ube.com/watch?v=iVURfHs2W3I&t=1797s.

160 Allan Scanlan interview, *Happy Michael Jackson Day*, https://www.youtube.com/watch?v =LGWvA-4cO_8.

161 Michael Jackson and sister Latoya interview at Encino home, Winter 1983, https://www. youtube160.com/watch?v=bwEbyaOpvY0.

162 Michael Jackson interview, *Get Music*, 2001, https://www.youtube.com/watch?v=heCJbo s7dfE.

163 Rory Kaplan interview, *Red Jackson Dance*, October 15, 2022, https://www.youtube.com/ watch?v=6IbFIoTcd14&t=2862s.

164 Michael Jackson interview, *Get Music*, 2001, https://www.youtube.com/watch?v=heCJbo s7dfE.

165 Ibid.

166 Michael Jackson interview, *Ebony/Jet*, 1987, https://www.youtube.com/watch?v=9hARx BrSsa8.

167 *Living with Michael Jackson*, directed by Julie Shaw.

168 Smallcombe, *Making Michael*, 107.

169 The Dangerous Deposition, 1994, https://www.youtube.com/watch?v=R_8djvUGre8.

170 Ibid.

171 Brad Buxer interview, *MJ Cast*, Episode 100, May 5, 2019, https://www.themjcast.com/e pisode-100-brad-buxer-special/.

172 Kevin Dorsey interview, *MJ Cast*, Episode 115, March 15, 2020, https://www.themjcast.c om/episode-115-kevin-dorsey-special/.

173 Smallcombe, *Making Michael*, 108.

174 Brad Buxer interview, *MJ Cast*, Episode 100, May 5, 2019, https://www.themjcast.com/e pisode-100-brad-buxer-special/.

175 Rob Hoffman interview, *MJ Cast*, Episode 30, May 6, 2016, https://www.themjcast.com/e pisode-030-rob-hoffman-special/.

176 Bill Whitfield interview, *MJ Book Club*, June 27, 2020, https://www.youtube.com/watch?v =5oYJVHb9BKU&t=3266s.

177 Brad Buxer interview, *Jackson.ch*, August 29, 2022, https://www.youtube.com/watch?v=r Ex3VhuE5iU.

178 Michael Jackson interview, *Get Music*, 2001, https://www.youtube.com/watch?v=heCJbo s7dfE.

179 Matt Forger interview, *MJ Cast*, Episode 150, December 22, 2022, https://www.themjcast. com/150-matt-forger-special-part-1/.

180 Vincent Paterson interview, *MJ Cast*, Episode 64, August 28, 2017, https://www.themjcas t.com/episode-064-vincent-paterson-special/.

181 Michael Jackson interview, *Get Music*, 2001, https://www.youtube.com/watch?v=heCJbo s7dfE.

182 Ibid.

183 Mazzola, "Michael Jackson: Take 2."

1993

184 Chuck Arnold, "How Michael Jackson Changed the Super Bowl Halftime Game in 1993: The Whole World Cared," *New York Post*, February 11, 2023, https://nypost.com/2023/02 /11/michael-jackson-changed-the-super-bowl-halftime-game-in-1993/.

185 Michael Jackson speech, 1993 Grammy Awards, https://www.youtube.com/watch?v=Vt4 aH3dypio.

186 Mary A. Fischer, "Was Michael Jackson Framed? The Untold Story," *GQ*, October 1994, https://mjjtruthnow.wordpress.com/2014/05/20/was-michael-jackson-framed-the-defi ning-1994-gq-article-by-mary-a-fischer-that-set-the-record-straight-on-the-1993-alleg ations/.

187 "Chandler Timeline," *Turning the Table on the Chandler Allegations*, April 20, 2014, https://tu rningthetableonthechandlerallegations.wordpress.com/2014/04/20/chandler-timeline/.

188 Fischer, "Was Michael Jackson Framed?"

189 June Chandler testimony, Michael Jackson child molestation trial court transcript, April 11, 2005.

190 Fischer, "Was Michael Jackson Framed?"

191 June Chandler testimony, Michael Jackson child molestation trial court transcript, April 11, 2005.

192 Brett Barnes interview, *MJ Cast*, Episode 145, June 13, 2022, https://www.themjcast.com/ 145-vindication-day-special-with-brett-barnes/.

193 Tim White, "Justice for Michael Jackson," *The Objective Standard*, Spring 2020.

194 Brad Sundberg interview, *The Hustle*, March 16, 2019, https://thehustle.podbean.com/e/b onus-brad-sundberg-technical-director-for-michael-jackson/.

195 Ibid.

196 "The Girl in the Video 'Smooth Criminal,'" *Noblemania*, July 29, 2013, https://www.noble mania.com/2013/07/the-girl-in-video-smooth-criminal-1988.html.

197 Kelley Parker interview with Steve Freiss, https://truemichaeljackson.webnode.cz/more- about-michael/kellie-parker-about-michael/.

198 Kelley Parker interview at Neverland, *RTL4*, July 6, 2009, https://www.youtube.com/wat ch?v=uOlVxk73jpM.

199 "The Girl in the Video 'Smooth Criminal,'" *Noblemania*, July 29, 2013, https://www.noble mania.com/2013/07/the-girl-in-video-smooth-criminal-1988.html.

200 Brad Sundberg interview, *The Hustle*, March 16, 2019, https://thehustle.podbean.com/e/b onus-brad-sundberg-technical-director-for-michael-jackson/.

201 Michael Jackson and Lisa Marie Presley interview with Dianne Sawyer, *Primetime*, June 14, 1995, https://www.youtube.com/watch?v=H5xxK7ad-zg.

202 Violet Gaitan interview, *MJ Cast*, Episode 149, November 6, 2022, https://www.themjcas t.com/149-violet-gaitan-booker-special/.

203 Fischer, "Was Michael Jackson Framed?"

204 June Chandler testimony, Michael Jackson child molestation trial court transcript, April 11, 2005.

205 David Nordahl interview, *Reflections on the Dance*.

206 *Square One*, directed by Danny Wu (Danny Wu, 2019), streaming video.

207 Fischer, "Was Michael Jackson Framed?"

208 June Chandler testimony, Michael Jackson child molestation trial court transcript, April 11, 2005.

209 Fischer, "Was Michael Jackson Framed?"

210 Evan Chandler and David Schwartz taped phone conversation, July 8, 1993, https://themi chaeljacksonallegationsblog.wordpress.com/2016/12/26/taped-phone-conversations-be tween-evan-chandler-and-david-schwartz-on-july-8-1993/.

211 Fischer, "Was Michael Jackson Framed?" and Wu, *Square One*.

212 Ibid.

213 Ibid.

214 Geraldine Hughes interview, *MJ Cast*, Episode 157, July 6, 2023, https://www.themjcast.c om/157-vindication-day-special-with-geraldine-hughes/.

215 Fischer, "Was Michael Jackson Framed?"

216 Wu, *Square One*.

217 Fischer, "Was Michael Jackson Framed?"

218 David Nordahl interview, *Reflections on the Dance*.

219 "The Chandlers' Monetary Demands," *The Michael Jackson Allegations*, December 26, 2016, https://themichaeljacksonallegationsblog.wordpress.com/2016/12/26/the-chandlers-m onetary-demands/.

220 Wu, *Square One*.

221 Fischer, "Was Michael Jackson Framed?"

222 Ibid.

223 Geraldine Hughes interview, *MJ Cast*, Episode 157, July 6, 2023, https://www.themjcast.com/157-vindication-day-special-with-geraldine-hughes/.

224 Taj Jackson interview, *Constantine Isaias*, January 2, 2020, https://www.youtube.com/watch?v=BRg5VUgP5Y0.

225 Fischer, "Was Michael Jackson Framed?"

226 Ibid.

227 Ibid.

228 Sonia Nazario, "Jackson Sued by Boy Who Alleged Sexual Molestation," *Los Angeles Times*, September 15, 1993, https://www.latimes.com/archives/la-xpm-1993-09-15-me-35320-story.html.

229 Brad Buxer interview, *MJ Cast*, Episode 100, May 5, 2019, https://www.themjcast.com/episode-100-brad-buxer-special/.

230 Fischer, "Was Michael Jackson Framed?"

231 Ibid.

232 Corey Feldman interview, *Today*, October 30, 2017, https://www.youtube.com/watch?v=uL_mA9nZBDc.

233 John Ziegler interview with Taj Jackson and Charles Thomson, September 29, 2019, https://www.youtube.com/watch?v=C72bM-KRDRw.

234 Jessica Cros, "While Jackson Tours, The Lawyers War," *Washington Post*, November 8, 1993, https://www.washingtonpost.com/archive/lifestyle/1993/11/08/while-jackson-tours-the-lawyers-war/6fed8ee1-73d6-4326-b5db-1198d372088d/.

235 Adam Sandler, "Jackson Told to Cooperate," *Variety*, November 23, 1993, https://variety.com/1993/biz/news/jackson-told-to-cooperate-in-civil-trial-116092/.

236 Geraldine Hughes, *Redemption: The Truth Behind the Michael Jackson Child Molestation Allegations* (Los Angeles, CA: Hughes Publishing, 2004), 133.

237 Sandler, "Jackson Told to Cooperate."

238 Wu, *Square One*.

239 David Nordahl interview, *Reflections on the Dance*.

240 Debbie Rowe testimony, Katherine Jackson v. AEG, https://www.teammichaeljackson.com/jackson-v-aeg-the-trial/.

241 Ibid.

242 Brad Buxer interview, *MJ Cast*, Episode 100, May 5, 2019, https://www.themjcast.com/episode-100-brad-buxer-special/.

243 Carol LaMere interview, *MJ Cast*, Episode 133, June 12, 2021, https://www.themjcast.com/133-vindication-day-special-with-carol-lamere/.

244 Brad Buxer interview, *MJ Cast*, Episode 100, May 5, 2019, https://www.themjcast.com/episode-100-brad-buxer-special/.

245 Jacksonallegations, "Did Jordan Chandler's description of Michael Jackson's penis match the photographs taken of the star's genitalia by the police?" *The Michael Jackson Allegations*, https://themichaeljacksonallegationsblog.wordpress.com/2016/12/26/did-jordan-chand lers-description-of-michael-jacksons-penis-match-the-photographs-taken-of-the-stars-genitalia-by-the-police/.

246 Michael Jackson Neverland Statement Post Police Body Search, December 1993, https://w ww.youtube.com/watch?v=w270PK4o2_c.

247 Violet Gaitan interview, *MJ Cast*, Episode 149, November 6, 2022, https://www.themjcas t.com/149-violet-gaitan-booker-special/.

248 Jacksonallegations, "Did Jordan Chandler's Description ...?" *The Michael Jackson Allegations*.

249 Jacksonallegations, "Did Jordan Chandler's Description ...?" *The Michael Jackson Allegations*.

250 "Boy's Lawyer Seeks Photos of Michael Jackson's Body," *Los Angeles Times*, January 5, 1994, https://www.latimes.com/archives/la-xpm-1994-01-05-me-8514-story.html.

251 Jim Newton, "Grand Jury Calls Michael Jackson's Mother to Testify," *Los Angeles Times*, March 16, 1994, https://www.latimes.com/archives/la-xpm-1994-03-16-me-34715-stor y.html.

252 "Jackson Deposition Delayed," *UPI*, January 14, 1994, https://www.upi.com/Archives/19 94/01/14/Jackson-deposition-delayed/5160758523600/.

253 Wu, *Square One*.

254 Rochelle Steinhaus, "Jackson Settlement from 1993 Allegations topped $20 million," *Court TV*, June 16, 2004, http://www.cnn.com/2004/LAW/06/16/michael.jackson/.

255 "Mr. Jackson's Memorandum in Support of Objection to Subpoena to Larry Feldman for Settlement Documents," Case No. 1133603, Superior Court of the State of California, for the County of Santa Barbra, Santa Maria Division, https://web.archive.org/web/2020031 8232646/http://www.sbscpublicaccess.org/docs/ctdocs/032205mjmemospprtobj.pdf.

256 "Report Says Jackson Wanted Insurance to Pay Teen Accuser," *Santa Cruz Sentinel*, Volume 137, Number 28, January 29, 1994, https://cdnc.ucr.edu/?a=d&d=SCS19940129.1.6&srpo s=30&e=———199-en—20—21-byDA-txt-txIN-%22michael+jackson%22——1994—-1.

257 Wu, *Square One*.

258 "Mr. Jackson's Memorandum in Support of Objection to Subpoena to Larry Feldman for Settlement Documents," Case No. 1133603, Superior Court of the State of California, for the County of Santa Barbara, Santa Maria Division, https://web.archive.org/web/202003 18232646/http://www.sbscpublicaccess.org/docs/ctdocs/032205mjmemospprtobj.pdf.

259 Fischer, "Was Michael Jackson Framed?"

260 Mazzola, "Michael Jackson: Take 2."

261 Fischer, "Was Michael Jackson Framed?"

262 Jacksonallegations, "The Settlement," *The Michael Jackson Allegations*, December 26, 2016, https://themichaeljacksonallegationsblog.wordpress.com/2016/12/26/the-settlement/.

263 Jacksonallegations, "Evan Chandler's 1996 Lawsuit Against Michael Jackson," *The Michael Jackson Allegations*, December 26, 2016, https://themichaeljacksonallegationsblog.wordpr ess.com/2016/12/26/evan-chandlers-1996-lawsuit-against-michael-jackson/.

264 Carol LaMere interview, *MJ Cast*, Episode 133, June 12, 2021, https://www.themjcast.co m/133-vindication-day-special-with-carol-lamere/.

265 Amanda Prahl, "Jordie Chandler, Michael Jackson's First Accuser, Hasn't Been Seen in Years," *Popsugar*, March 21, 2019, https://www.popsugar.com/entertainment/who-jordy-chandler-where-he-2019-45929172.

266 June Chandler testimony, Michael Jackson child molestation trial court transcript, April 11, 2005.

267 September 23, 2004 FBI file, Case ID # 305B-LA-239204, https://vault.fbi.gov/Michael%20Jackson/Michael%20Jackson%20Part%2007%20of%2008/view.

268 Tom Mesereau Harvard Law School speech, November 29, 2005, https://www.youtube.c om/watch?v=-eSC997_HH0.

269 Wu, *Square One.*

270 Jordan Chandler v. Evan Chandler, Superior Court of New Jersey, Appellate Division, Docket No. A-0422-05T1, https://law.justia.com/cases/new-jersey/appellate-division-u npublished/2006/a0422-05-opn.html and https://themichaeljacksonallegationsblog.files. wordpress.com/2016/12/jordan-versus-evan-chandler-2006.pdf.

271 David Jones, "Killed by the Curse of Michael Jackson: What Drove the Father of Jordy Chandler to Put a Gun to his Head?" *The Daily Mail*, November 20, 2009, https://www.da ilymail.co.uk/tvshowbiz/article-1229622/Killed-curse-Michael-Jackson-What-drove-fat her-Jordy-Chandler-gun-head.html.

272 "Prosecutor Says Law Won't Allow Jackson to Pay Off Accuser Before Trial," *Associated Press*, November 20, 2003, https://www.deseret.com/2003/11/20/19796963/prosecutor-says-law-won-t-allow-jackson-to-pay-off-accuser-before-trial.

273 Raymond Chandler, *All That Glitters: The Crime and the Cover-Up* (Chicago, IL: Midpoint Trade Books, 2004), 128.

274 Michael Jackson Neverland Statement Post Police Body Search, December 1993, https://w ww.youtube.com/watch?v=w270PK4o2_c.

THE RESPONSE

275 Michael Jackson and Lisa Marie Presley interview with Dianne Sawyer, *Primetime*, June 14, 1995, https://www.youtube.com/watch?v=H5xxK7ad-zg.

276 Jacksonallegations, "Evan Chandler's 1996 Lawsuit Against Michael Jackson," *The Michael Jackson Allegations*.

277 Allan Scanlan interview, *Red Jackson Dance*, December 17, 2022, https://www.youtube.co m/watch?v=Hd3nDxLqtFY&t=4813s.

278 Allan Scanlan interview, *Happy Michael Jackson Day*, Part 1, https://www.youtube.com/watch?v=4viLuS9un0Q.

THE QUIET YEARS

279 Allan Scanlan interview, *Happy Michael Jackson Day*, Part 2, https://www.youtube.com/watch?v=ikpsF16GkCs.

280 Smallcombe, *Making Michael*, 306.

281 Ibid., 287.

282 Ibid., 271.

283 Brad Buxer interview, *MJ Cast*, Episode 100, May 5, 2019, https://www.themjcast.com/episode-100-brad-buxer-special/.

284 Smallcombe, *Making Michael*, 275.

285 Ibid., 302.

286 Ibid., 293.

287 Oxford University speech, 2001, https://www.youtube.com/watch?v=PkElyPTY1u8.

288 "Was Michael Jackson Almost in WTC on 9/11?" *Today*, https://www.today.com/popculture/was-michael-jackson-almost-wtc-9-11-2d80555837.

289 Lisa Marie Presley interview, "Lisa Marie Presley Opens up about Michael Jackson," *Oprah*, October 21, 2010, https://www.oprah.com/oprahshow/lisa-marie-presley-opens-up-about-michael-jackson/all and Lester Fabian Brathwaite, "Remember Lisa Marie Presley and Michael Jackson's Turbulent 2-year Marriage," *Entertainment Weekly*, January 12, 2023.

290 Smallcombe, *Making Michael*, 215.

291 Jimmy Jam interview, *Go with Elmo*, June 14, 2023, https://www.youtube.com/watch?v=2R4utgYvHdY.

292 Lisa Marie Presley interview, "Lisa Marie Presley Opens up about Michael Jackson," *Oprah*, October 21, 2010, https://www.oprah.com/oprahshow/lisa-marie-presley-opens-up-about-michael-jackson/all and Lester Fabian Brathwaite, "Remember Lisa Marie Presley and Michael Jackson's Turbulent 2-year Marriage," *Entertainment Weekly*, January 12, 2023.

293 Katherine Jackson testimony, Katherine Jackson v. AEG, https://www.teammichaeljackson.com/jackson-v-aeg-the-trial/.

294 David Nordahl interview, *Reflections on the Dance*.

295 Paris Jackson interview, *Steve-O's Wild Ride!*, September 8, 2022, https://www.youtube.com/watch?v=rI4AkTc-wOc.

296 David Nordahl interview, *Reflections on the Dance*.

297 Paris Jackson interview with Naomi Campbell, *Naomi*, March 30, 2021, https://www.youtube.com/watch?v=GPhmZWah1b4&t=1s.

298 Prince Jackson interview, *Remembering Michael*, 2012, https://www.youtube.com/watch?v=ZSyv7XRaZsw.

299 Prince Jackson interview, *WhereistheBuzz TV*, August 25, 2022, https://www.youtube.com /watch?v=TdwG_P8xRaQ.

300 Taryll Jackson interview, *MJ Cast*, Episode 101, May 18, 2019.

301 Michael Jackson interview, *Geraldo Rivera*, 2005, https://www.youtube.com/watch?v=7u-Hl_K5nqQ.

NOT AGAIN

302 Jenny Winings interview, *MJ Cast*, Episode 104, June 25, 2019, https://www.themjcast.co m/episode-104-june-25th-special-with-jenny-winings/.

303 Arvizo rebuttal video outtakes, "Michael Jackson: A Case for Innocence," Larry Nimmer documentary, https://www.youtube.com/watch?v=llLQEi4NMxI.

304 Carol LaMere interview, *MJ Cast*, Episode 133, June 12, 2021, https://www.themjcast.co m/133-vindication-day-special-with-carol-lamere/.

305 Jacksonallegations, "An Introduction of the Arvizo Family and How Their Relationship with Michael Jackson Started," *The Michael Jackson Allegations*, December 26, 2016, https://t hemichaeljacksonallegationsblog.wordpress.com/2016/12/26/an-introduction-of-the-ar vizo-family-and-how-their-relationship-with-michael-jackson-started/.

306 *Living with Michael Jackson*, directed by Julie Shaw.

307 Jacksonallegations, "An Introduction of the Arvizo Family...," *The Michael Jackson Allegations*.

308 *Living with Michael Jackson*, directed by Julie Shaw.

309 Lisa Marie Presley interview, *Oprah Winfrey*, October 21, 2010, https://michaeljacksoneli sapresley.blogspot.com/2015/01/transcript-lisa-marie-on-oprah-winfrey.html.

310 Scott Ross interview, *MJ Cast*, Episode 33, June 12, 2016, https://www.themjcast.com/epi sode-033-vindication-day-special-with-scott-ross/.

311 Jacksonallegations, "An Introduction of the Arvizo Family ...," *The Michael Jackson Allegations*.

312 Aphrodite Jones, *Michael Jackson Conspiracy*, (Bloomington, IN: Aphrodite Jones Books, 2007), 60, 117.

313 "Michael Jackson: A Case for Innocence," Larry Nimmer documentary, https://www.yout ube.com/watch?v=llLQEi4NMxI.

314 Tom Mesereau interview, *MJ Cast*, Episode 10, June 13, 2015, https://www.themjcast.co m/episode-010-vindication-day-10th-anniversary-special-with-tom-mesereau/.

315 "Michael Jackson: A Case for Innocence," Larry Nimmer documentary.

316 Jones, *Michael Jackson Conspiracy*, 115.

317 Jones, *Michael Jackson Conspiracy*, 86, 87, 110.

318 Jacksonallegations, "Lawyers Being Hired and the Formation of the Allegations," *The Michael Jackson Allegations*, December 17, 2016, https://themichaeljacksonallegationsblog.

wordpress.com/2016/12/27/lawyers-being-hired-and-the-formation-of-the-allegations
/.

319 Violet Gaitan interview, *MJ Cast*, Episode 149, November 6, 2022, https://www.themjcas
t.com/149-violet-gaitan-booker-special/.

320 Jacksonallegations, "Lawyers Being Hired …," *The Michael Jackson Allegations*.

321 Michael Jackson interview, *60 Minutes*, December 25, 2003, https://www.youtube.com/w
atch?v=-GF2JUe-2Is.

322 Statement of Probable Cause, November 17, 2003, Superior Court of California, County
of Santa Barbara, https://themichaeljacksonallegationsblog.files.wordpress.com/2016/12
/plugin-111703stmtpc.pdf.

323 Felony Complaint, The People of the State of California v. Michael Joe Jackson, DA No.
03-12-098996, December 18, 2003, https://themichaeljacksonallegationsblog.files.wordp
ress.com/2016/12/121803complaint_initial-charges.pdf.

324 "Michael Jackson: A Case for Innocence," Larry Nimmer documentary.

325 Gavin Arvizo testimony, Michael Jackson child molestation trial court transcript, March
14, 2005.

326 Charles Thomson interview, *MJ Cast*, Episode 58, January 21, 2017, https://www.youtub
e.com/watch?v=5POaTSQfSg8.

327 "Michael Jackson: A Case for Innocence," Larry Nimmer documentary.

328 Janet Arvizo testimony, Michael Jackson child molestation trial court transcript, April 18,
2005.

329 Gavin Arvizo testimony, Michael Jackson child molestation trial court transcript, March
14, 2005.

330 Brad Buxer interview, *Jackson.ch*, August 29, 2022, https://www.youtube.com/watch?y=r
Ex3VhuF5iU.

331 Aphrodite Jones interview, *MJ Cast*, Episode 81, June 13, 2018, https://www.themjcast.co
m/episode-081-vindication-day-special-with-aphrodite-jones/.

332 Jones, *The Michael Jackson Conspiracy*, 57.

333 Jay Leno testimony, Michael Jackson child molestation trial court transcript, May 24,
2005.

334 Jones, *The Michael Jackson Conspiracy*, 111.

335 Ibid., 150–153.

336 Ibid., 88.

337 Ibid., 198.

338 "Michael Jackson: A Case for Innocence," Larry Nimmer documentary.

339 Jones, *The Michael Jackson Conspiracy*, 87.

340 "Michael Jackson: A Case for Innocence," Larry Nimmer documentary.

341 White, "Justice for Michael Jackson" and Tom Mesereau interview, *On Second Thought*, December 13, 2010, https://www.youtube.com/watch?v=x_uSuUzqby8.

342 Jury interview, *Good Morning America*, June 14, 2005, https://www.youtube.com/watch?v=EhTf4IFS3Zs.

343 Jury interview, *Larry King Live*, June 13, 2005, https://www.youtube.com/watch?v=s-AtRZ74ZjU&t=721s.

344 Paul Rodrigues interview with Aphrodite Jones, November 15, 2012, https://www.youtube.com/watch?v=RSht7eNpHSA.

345 Jury Press Conference, June 13, 2005, https://www.youtube.com/watch?v=dnn2j_XUXvw&t=869s.

346 Jacksonallegations, "The Prosecution Witnesses, Ralph Chacon, Kassim Abdool, Adrian McManus," *The Michael Jackson Allegations*, December 26, 2016, https://themichaeljacksonallegationsblog.wordpress.com/2016/12/26/the-prosecutions-witnesses-ralph-chacon-kassim-abdool-and-adrian-mcmanus/.

347 Jacksonallegations, "Blanca Francia," May 12, 2018, https://themichaeljacksonallegationsblog.wordpress.com/2018/05/12/wades-witnesses-part-2/.

348 Tom Mesereau interview, *MJ Cast*, Episode 10, June 13, 2015, https://www.themjcast.com/episode-010-vindication-day-10th-anniversary-special-with-tom-mesereau/.

349 Ibid.

350 Brett Barnes interview, *MJ Cast*, Episode 145, June 13, 2022, https://www.themjcast.com/145-vindication-day-special-with-brett-barnes/.

351 Kerry Anderson interview, *MJ Cast*, Episode 5, April 10, 2015, https://www.youtube.com/watch?v=7HeFNxRpbOo.

352 Tom Mesereau interview, *MJ Cast*, Episode 10, June 13, 2015, https://www.themjcast.com/episode-010-vindication-day-10th-anniversary-special-with-tom-mesereau/.

353 Scott Ross interview, *MJ Cast*, Episode 33, June 12, 2016, https://www.themjcast.com/episode-033-vindication-day-special-with-scott-ross/.

354 Brad Buxer interview, *MJ Cast*, Episode 100, May 5, 2019, https://www.themjcast.com/episode-100-brad-buxer-special/.

355 Violet Gaitan interview, *MJ Cast*, Episode 149, November 6, 2022, https://www.themjcast.com/149-violet-gaitan-booker-special/.

356 David Nordahl interview, *Reflections on the Dance*.

357 Tom Mesereau interview, *William Wagner*, January 17, 2008, https://www.youtube.com/watch?v=F0_Ict_GhPY.

358 Aphrodite Jones interview, *MJ Cast*, Episode 81, June 13, 2018, https://www.themjcast.com/episode-081-vindication-day-special-with-aphrodite-jones/.

359 Jones, *The Michael Jackson Conspiracy*, 87.

360 Jury Interview, *Good Morning America*, June 14, 2005, https://www.youtube.com/watch?v=EhTf4IFS3Zs.

361 Susan Yu interview, *Michael Jackson: The Life of an Icon World Premiere*, https://www.youtube.com/watch?v=2_HY74YEnhA&t=552s.

362 Jury Interview, *Good Morning America*, June 14, 2005, https://www.youtube.com/watch?v=EhTf4IFS3Zs.

363 Tom Mesereau interview, *MJ Cast*, Episode 10, June 13, 2015, https://www.themjcast.com/episode-010-vindication-day-10th-anniversary-special-with-tom-mesereau/.

364 Kerry Anderson interview, *MJ Cast*, Episode 5, April 10, 2015, https://www.youtube.com/watch?v=7HeFNxRpbOo.

365 Allan Scanlan interview, *MJ Cast*, Episode 107, August 24, 2019, https://www.themjcast.com/episode-107-allan-big-al-scanlan-special/.

366 Charles Thomson interview, *MJ Cast*, 262, August 7, 2017, https://www.themjcast.com/episode-062-they-didnt-need-an-expert-to-say-that/.

THE RECOVERY

367 Tom Mesereau interview, *MJ Cast*, Episode 10, June 13, 2015, https://www.themjcast.com/episode-010-vindication-day-10th-anniversary-special-with-tom-mesereau/.

368 Violet Gaitan interview, *MJ Cast*, Episode 149, November 6, 2022, https://www.themjcast.com/149-violet-gaitan-booker-special/.

369 Aphrodite Jones interview, *MJ Cast*, Episode 81, June 13, 2018, https://www.themjcast.com/episode-081-vindication-day-special-with-aphrodite-jones/.

370 Kerry Anderson interview, *MJ Cast*, Episode 5, April 10, 2015, https://www.youtube.com/watch?v=7HeFNxRpbOo.

371 Ibid.

372 Carol LaMere interview, *MJ Cast*, Episode 133, June 12, 2021, https://www.themjcast.com/133-vindication-day-special-with-carol-lamere/.

373 Patrick Treacy interview, September 26, 2010, https://www.youtube.com/watch?v=OMW7PXqU2Vg.

374 Ibid.

375 Patrick Treacy interview, September 26, 2010, https://www.youtube.com/watch?v=iPEXT8qEc-g.

376 World Music Awards 2006 10th Anniversary Special, *MJ Cast*, Episode 44, December 24, 2016, https://www.youtube.com/watch?v=iw3j6Mb_mHI.

377 Ibid.

378 Mike Garcia Interview, *King Jordan Radio*, April 26, 2014, https://www.youtube.com/watch?v=R8IZJNlOIKk.

379 Bill Whitfield, Javon Beard, and Tanner Colby, *Remember the Time: Protecting Michael Jackson in His Final Days* (New York, NY: Hachette Books, 2014), 145.

380 Brad Buxer interview, *MJ Cast*, Episode 100, May 5, 2019, https://www.themjcast.com/episode-100-brad-buxer-special/.

381 Whitfield, Beard, and Colby, *Remember the Time*, 116, 268.

382 Ibid., 125.

383 Ibid., 121.

384 Mike Garcia interview, *Red Jackson Dance*, January 14, 2023, https://www.youtube.com/watch?v=ccJqHeZ_fa0.

385 Whitfield, Beard, and Colby, *Remember the Time*, 121.

386 Bill Whitfield interview, *MJRadioNet*, February 16, 2021, https://www.youtube.com/watch?v=MrTryG3Bydk&t=4981s.

387 Whitfield, Beard, and Colby, *Remember the Time*, 130–131.

388 Rory Kaplan interview, *Red Jackson Dance*, October 15, 2022, https://www.youtube.com/watch?v=6IbFIoTcd14&t=2862s.

389 Prince Jackson speaking about compassion, Instagram Live, March 24, 2021, https://www.youtube.com/watch?v=1JrrYDNrgE0.

390 Mike Garcia interview, *Red Jackson Dance*, January 14, 2023, https://www.youtube.com/watch?v=ccJqHeZ_fa0.

391 Bill Whitfield interview, *MJ Book Club*, May 10, 2020, https://www.youtube.com/watch?v=_qeKUWYCeI8.

392 Aileen Medalla interview, *MJ Cast*, Episode 132, June 5, 2021, https://www.themjcast.com/132-aileen-medalla-special/.

393 Whitfield, Beard, and Colby, *Remember the Time*, 198.

394 Ibid., 201.

395 Bill Whitfield interview, *MJ Book Club*, June 27, 2020, https://www.youtube.com/watch?v=5oYJVHb9BKU&t=3266s.

396 Bill Whitfield interview, *MJ Book Club*, May 10, 2020, https://www.youtube.com/watch?v=_qeKUWYCeI8.

397 Dr. Allan Metzger testimony, Katherine Jackson v. AEG trial, https://www.teammichaeljackson.com/jackson-v-aeg-the-trial/.

398 Whitfield, Beard, and Colby, *Remember the Time*, 265.

MICHAEL'S PASSING

399 Smallcombe, *Making Michael*, 339–340.

400 Ibid., 343.

401 Ibid., 343.

402 Ibid., 344–345.

403 Randy Phillips testimony, Katherine Jackson v. AEG, https://www.teammichaeljackson.com/jackson-v-aeg-the-trial/.

404 Randy Phillips testimony, Conrad Murray criminal trial, https://www.youtube.com/watch?v=vTFXmUHTrjo&list=PLh4Z38to3Hf62pm_lsg60RJYWnsT7Tuzl&index=112.

405 Smallcombe, *Making Michael*, 344–345.

406 Randy Phillips testimony, Katherine Jackson v. AEG, https://www.teammichaeljackson.com/jackson-v-aeg-the-trial/.

407 Randy Phillips testimony, Conrad Murray criminal trial, https://www.youtube.com/watch?v=vTFXmUHTrjo&list=PLh4Z38to3Hf62pm_lsg60RJYWnsT7Tuzl&index=112.

408 Smallcombe, *Making Michael*, 344–345.

409 Dr. Allan Metzger testimony, Katherine Jackson v. AEG trial, https://www.teammichaeljackson.com/jackson-v-aeg-the-trial/.

410 David Nordahl interview, *Reflections on the Dance*.

411 Jennifer Batten interview, *Red Jackson Dance*, August 7, 2022, https://www.youtube.com/watch?v=lQN1cRK3n-4&t=1297s.

412 Dr. Allan Metzger testimony, Katherine Jackson v. AEG trial, https://www.teammichaeljackson.com/jackson-v-aeg-the-trial/.

413 Ibid.

414 Michael Prince interview, *MJ Cast*, Episode 52, March 19, 2017, https://www.themjcast.com/episode-052-michael-prince-special/.

415 David Nordahl interview, *Reflections on the Dance*, August 19, 2013, https://www.youtube.com/watch?v=dUChOzzyJ5E.

416 David Nordahl interview, *Reflections on the Dance*.

417 Dr. Charles Czeisler testimony, Katherine Jackson v. AEG, https://www.teammichaeljackson.com/jackson-v-aeg-the-trial/.

418 Karen Faye testimony, Katherine Jackson v. AEG, https://www.teammichaeljackson.com/jackson-v-aeg-the-trial/.

419 Dr. Cherlyn Lee testimony, Katherine Jackson v. AEG, https://www.teammichaeljackson.com/jackson-v-aeg-the-trial/.

420 Ibid.

421 Dr. Cherlyn Lee testimony, Dr. Murray criminal trial, https://www.youtube.com/watch?v=oRofkxHO5FE&list=PLh4Z38to3Hf62pm_lsg60RJYWnsT7Tuzl&index=111.

422 Dr. Cherlyn Lee testimony, Katherine Jackson v. AEG, https://www.teammichaeljackson.com/jackson-v-aeg-the-trial/.

423 Ibid.

424 Debbie Rowe testimony, Katherine Jackson v. AEG, https://www.teammichaeljackson.co
m/jackson-v-aeg-the-trial/.

425 Dr. Allan Metzger testimony, Katherine Jackson v. AEG trial, https://www.teammichaelj
ackson.com/jackson-v-aeg-the-trial/.

426 Dr. William B. Van Valin II testimony, Katherine Jackson v. AEG trial, https://www.team
michaeljackson.com/jackson-v-aeg-the-trial/.

427 Michael Jackson interview, *Barbra Walters*, September 7, 1997, https://www.youtube.com
/watch?v=gFIjGn4yA6c.

428 Michael Prince interview, *MJ Cast*, Episode 52, March 19, 2017, https://www.themjcast.c
om/episode-052-michael-prince-special/

429 Michael Jackson interview, *Get Music*, 2001, https://www.youtube.com/watch?v=heCJbo
s7dfE.

430 Dr. Cherlyn Lee testimony, Katherine Jackson v. AEG, https://www.teammichaeljackson.
com/jackson-v-aeg-the-trial/.

431 Ibid.

432 Ibid.

433 Email from Paul Gongaware to Michael Amir Williams, May 6, https://www.psbr.law/w
p-content/uploads/2020/12/Exhibit-175-GONGAWARE-9887.pdf.

434 Prince Jackson testimony, Katherine Jackson v. AEG, https://www.teammichaeljackson.c
om/jackson-v-aeg-the-trial/.

435 Lou Ferrigno interview, *Larry King Live*, July 3, 2009, https://www.youtube.com/watch?v
=HTIoxTrKP84.

436 Lou Ferrigno interview, *Associated Press*, June 30, 2009, https://www.youtube.com/watch
?v=oepchWF8ijo.

437 Kai Chase interview, *Today Show*, July 30, 2009, https://www.youtube.com/watch?v=9GX
zWLYp1-0, https://www.youtube.com/watch?v=BBjA0X4FtkY, and https://www.youtu
be.com/watch?v=BBjA0X4FtkY.

438 *Michael Jackson's This Is It*, directed by Kenny Ortega (Sony Pictures Television, 2009),
DVD.

439 Judith Hill interview, *MJ Cast*, Episode 84, July 13, 2018, https://www.themjcast.com/epi
sode-084-judith-hill-special/.

440 Travis Payne interview, *MJ Cast*, Episode 124, October 23, 2020, https://www.themjcast.c
om/124-travis-payne-special/.

441 Judith Hill interview, *MJ Cast*, Episode 84, July 13, 2018, https://www.themjcast.com/epi
sode-084-judith-hill-special/.

442 Alif Sankey testimony, Katherine Jackson v. AEG, https://www.teammichaeljackson.com
/alif-sankey-associate-producer-this-is-it/.

443 Email from Kenny Ortega to Paul Gongaware, June 14, 2009, https://www.psbr.law/wp-content/uploads/2020/12/Exhibit-255-1.pdf.

444 Email from Paul Gongaware to Kenny Ortega, June 14, 2009, https://www.psbr.law/wp-content/uploads/2020/12/Exhibit-263-AEGL-32604-32605.pdf.

445 Randy Phillips testimony, Katherine Jackson v. AEG, https://www.teammichaeljackson.com/alif-sankey-associate-producer-this-is-it/.

446 Prince Jackson testimony, Katherine Jackson v. AEG trial, https://www.teammichaeljackson.com/jackson-v-aeg-the-trial/.

447 Kai Chase testimony, Katherine Jackson v. AEG trial, https://www.teammichaeljackson.com/jackson-v-aeg-the-trial/.

448 Email from Kenny Ortega to Randy Phillips, June 20, 2009, https://www.psbr.law/wp-content/uploads/2020/12/Exhibit-298-KO-716-719.pdf.

449 Email from John Houghdahl to Randy Phillips, June 19, 2009, Paul Gongaware testimony, Katherine Jackson v. AEG, https://www.teammichaeljackson.com/jackson-v-aeg-the-trial/.

450 Kenny Ortega testimony, Katherine Jackson v. AEG, https://www.teammichaeljackson.com/jackson-v-aeg-the-trial/.

451 Kenny Ortega testimony, Conrad Murray criminal trial, https://www.youtube.com/watch?v=BYVDasdko2o&list=PLh4Z38to3Hf62pm_lsg60RJYWnsT7Tuzl.

452 Karen Faye testimony, Katherine Jackson v. AEG, https://www.teammichaeljackson.com/jackson-v-aeg-the-trial/.

453 Kai Chase testimony, Katherine Jackson v. AEG, https://www.teammichaeljackson.com/jackson-v-aeg-the-trial/.

454 Ibid.

455 Prince Jackson testimony, Katherine Jackson v. AEG, https://www.teammichaeljackson.com/jackson-v-aeg-the-trial/.

456 Email from Randy Phillips to Kenny Ortega, June 20, 2009, https://www.psbr.law/wp-content/uploads/2020/12/Exhibit-298-KO-716-719.pdf.

457 Kenny Ortega testimony, Conrad Murray criminal trial, https://www.youtube.com/watch?v=BYVDasdko2o&list=PLh4Z38to3Hf62pm_lsg60RJYWnsT7Tuzl.

458 Kenny Ortega testimony, Katherine Jackson v. AEG, https://www.teammichaeljackson.com/jackson-v-aeg-the-trial/.

459 Randy Phillips testimony, Katherine Jackson v. AEG, https://www.teammichaeljackson.com/jackson-v-aeg-the-trial/.

460 Dr. Cherlyn Lee testimony, Katherine Jackson v. AEG, https://www.teammichaeljackson.com/jackson-v-aeg-the-trial/.

461 Dr. Cheryln Lee testimony, Conrad Murray criminal trial, https://www.youtube.com/watch?v=oRofkxH05FE&list=PLh4Z38to3Hf62pm_lsg60RJYWnsT7Tuzl&index=111.

462 Dr. Cherlyn Lee testimony, Katherine Jackson v. AEG, https://www.teammichaeljackson. com/jackson-v-aeg-the-trial/.

463 Kenny Ortega testimony, Katherine Jackson v. AEG, https://www.teammichaeljackson.c om/jackson-v-aeg-the-trial/.

464 Ibid.

465 Ibid.

466 Dr. Charles Czeisler testimony, Katherine Jackson v. AEG, https://www.teammichaeljack son.com/jackson-v-aeg-the-trial/.

467 Ibid.

468 Ibid.

469 Sade Anding testimony, Conrad Murray criminal trial, https://www.youtube.com/watch? v=aUqwl2zMYBs&list=PLh4Z38to3Hf62pm_lsg60RJYWnsT7Tuzl&index=57.

470 Kai Chase testimony, Conrad Murray criminal trial, https://www.youtube.com/watch?v =oworopXrTIc.

471 Michael Amir Williams testimony, Conrad Murray criminal trial, https://www.youtube.c om/watch?v=8mLM9grZHdQ&list=PLh4Z38to3Hf62pm_lsg60RJYWnsT7Tuzl&index= 11.

472 Alberto Alvarez testimony, Conrad Murray criminal trial, https://www.youtube.com/wat ch?v=-lNST8BH1Dw&list=PLh4Z38to3Hf62pm_lsg60RJYWnsT7Tuzl.

473 Conrad Murray sentencing, https://www.youtube.com/watch?v=rAhCOtX_2rg&list=PL h4Z38to3Hf62pm_lsg60RJYWnsT7Tuzl&index=140.

474 Michael Jackson slurred speech recorded by Conrad Murray on May 10, Conrad Murray criminal trial, https://www.youtube.com/watch?v=B1PE7MipD54.

475 Prosecution's Closing Arguments, Conrad Murray trial, https://www.youtube.com/watc h?v=oBd_KUsGj0I&list=PLh4Z38to3Hf62pm_lsg60RJYWnsT7Tuzl&index=136.

476 Shawn Trell testimony, Katherine Jackson v. AEG, https://www.teammichaeljackson.co m/shawn-trell-general-counsel-for-aeg-live-2/.

477 Samantha K. Brooks and Neil Greenburg, "Psychological Impact of Being Wrongly Accused of Criminal Offenses: A Systematic Literature Review," *Media, Science, and the Law*, August 17, 2020, https://journals.sagepub.com/doi/10.1177/0025802420949069.

478 "The Suffering of the Wrongfully Accused," *FACTUK*, https://factuk.org/how-to-cope/th e-suffering-of-the-wrongfully-accused/.

479 Smallcombe, *Making Michael*, 367.

480 Judith Hill interview, *MJ Cast*, Episode 84, July 13, 2018, https://www.themjcast.com/epi sode-084-judith-hill-special/.

481 TJ Jackson interview, *MJ Cast*, Episode 126, December 18, 2020, https://www.themjcast.c om/126-tj-jackson-special/.

482 Taj Jackson interview, *Constantine Isaias*, January 2, 2020, https://www.youtube.com/watch?v=BRg5VUgP5Y0.

483 Dr. Patrick Treacy interview, Reflections on the Dance, September 26, 2010, https://www.youtube.com/watch?v=2MWeRt_br9s.

484 "The Girl in the Video 'Smooth Criminal,'" *Noblemania*, July 29, 2013, https://www.noblemania.com/2013/07/the-girl-in-video-smooth-criminal-1988.html.

485 Violet Gaitan interview, *MJ Cast*, Episode 149, November 6, 2022, https://www.themjcast.com/149-violet-gaitan-booker-special/.

486 Allan Scanlan interview, *MJ Cast*, Episode 107, August 24, 2019, https://www.themjcast.com/episode-107-allan-big-al-scanlan-special/.

487 Dr. Cheryln Lee testimony, Katherine Jackson v. AEG, https://www.teammichaeljackson.com/jackson-v-aeg-the-trial/.

488 Marlon Jackson at Michael Jackson's memorial, https://www.youtube.com/watch?v=g6sGAVU5XmY.

NO RESTING IN PEACE

489 Wesley Morris, "Michael Jackson Cast a Spell. 'Leaving Neverland' Breaks It," *New York Times*, February 28, 2019, https://www.nytimes.com/2019/02/28/arts/television/michael-jackson-leaving-neverland.html.

490 Maureen Dowd, "The King of Pop—and Perversion," *New York Times*, February 16, 2019, https://www.nytimes.com/2019/02/16/opinion/sunday/michael-jackson-leaving-neverland.html.

491 Michael Barbaro, "Reckoning with the Real Michael Jackson," *New York Times*, March 8, 2019, https://www.nytimes.com/2019/03/08/podcasts/the-daily/michael-jackson-abuse-leaving-neverland.html.

492 Melanie McFarland, "Letting Go of Michael Jackson: 'Leaving Neverland' Wakes us from a False Dream," *Salon*, March 3, 2019, https://www.salon.com/2019/03/03/letting-go-of-michael-jackson-leaving-neverland-wakes-us-from-a-false-dream/.

493 Greg Tate, Alexis Petridis, Lyndsey Winship, Priya Elan, Chuck Klosterman, Laura Snapes, and Simran Hans, "Too Big to Cancel? Can we still listen to Michael Jackson?" *The Guardian*, March 1, 2019, https://www.theguardian.com/music/2019/mar/01/leaving-neverland-is-it-still-ok-to-listen-to-michael-jackson.

494 Jacksonallegations, "The Civil Lawsuit," May 12, 2018, *The Michael Jackson Allegations*, https://themichaeljacksonallegationsblog.wordpress.com/2018/05/12/the-litigation-part-2/.

495 White, "Justice for Michael Jackson."

496 Jacksonallegations, "Blanca Francia," *The Michael Jackson Allegations*, May 12, 2018, https://themichaeljacksonallegationsblog.wordpress.com/2018/05/12/wades-witnesses-part-2/.

497 Wade Robson testimony, Michael Jackson Child Molestation Trial, May 5, 2005, https://t hemichaeljacksonallegationsblog.wordpress.com/the-court-transcripts/.

498 "Lies of Leaving Neverland Full Movie," August 13, 2019, https://www.youtube.com/wat ch?v=CXOfz1YkWeA&t=2s.

499 Jacksonallegations, "A Failed Prophecy," May 12, 2018, *The Michael Jackson Allegations*, https://themichaeljacksonallegationsblog.wordpress.com/2018/05/12/robsons-route-to-changing-his-story-part-4/.

500 Liam McEwan, "Leaving Neverland Debunked!" April 9, 2019, https://www.youtube.com /watch?v=ssGZCZj88Cg.

501 Ibid.

502 Jacksonallegations, "A Book and a Lawsuit," May 12, 2018, *The Michael Jackson Allegations*, https://themichaeljacksonallegationsblog.wordpress.com/2018/05/12/robsons-route-to-changing-his-story-part-9/.

503 Ibid.

504 Brett Barnes tweet, May 8, 2013, https://twitter.com/IAmBrettBarnes/status/332153562 991837184.

505 McEwan, "Leaving Neverland Debunked!"

506 Wade Robson deposition, December 12, 2016, *The Michael Jackson Allegations*, https://the michaeljacksonallegationsblog.files.wordpress.com/2018/06/wade-robson-deposition-e xtracts.pdf.

507 McEwan, "Leaving Neverland Debunked!"

508 Jacksonallegations, "A Master of Deception: Then or Now?" *The Michael Jackson Allegations*, May 12, 2018, https://themichaeljacksonallegationsblog.wordpress.com/2018/05/12/ro bsons-route-to-changing-his-story-part-2/.

509 Jacksonallegations, "A Book and a Lawsuit," May 12, 2018, *The Michael Jackson Allegations*, https://themichaeljacksonallegationsblog.wordpress.com/2018/05/12/robsons-route-to-changing-his-story-part-9/.

510 White, "Justice for Michael Jackson."

511 Jacksonallegations, "The Probate Court Case (Creditor's Claim)," *The Michael Jackson Allegations*, May 12, 2018, https://themichaeljacksonallegationsblog.wordpress.com/2018 /05/12/the-litigation-part-1/.

512 Jacksonallegations, "The Civil Lawsuit," *The Michael Jackson Allegations*, May 12, 2018, https://themichaeljacksonallegationsblog.wordpress.com/2018/05/12/the-litigation-par t-2/.

513 White, "Justice for Michael Jackson."

514 Damien Shields, "Leaving Neverland Exposed: The Devil is in the Detail," https://erikbuy s.files.wordpress.com/2019/07/leaving-neverland-exposed-damien-shields.pdf.

515 Ibid and MJJJustice Project, "Debunking James Safechuck's Leaving Neverland Fiction," February 17, 2019, https://mjjjusticeproject.wordpress.com/2019/02/17/debunking-jam es-safechucks-leaving-neverland-fiction/.

516 Ibid.

517 Ibid.

518 Melody Chiu, "New Child Sex Abuse Claims Filed Against Michael Jackson," *People*, August 7, 2014, https://people.com/crime/new-child-sex-abuse-claims-filed-against-michael-ja ckson/.

519 Ibid.

520 McEwan, "Leaving Neverland Debunked!"

521 Charles Tomson interview, Free Speech Broadcasting, April 14, 2019, https://www.youtu be.com/watch?v=OL3rzFJn9tU&t=2502s.

522 Fischer, "Was Michael Jackson Framed?"

523 Jones, *Michael Jackson Conspiracy*, 60, 117.

CONCLUSION

524 Rick Porter, "'Leaving Neverland' Draws HBO's Third-Largest Doc Audience in a Decade," *The Hollywood Reporter*, March 5, 2019, https://www.hollywoodreporter.com/tv/tv-news /leaving-neverland-ratings-third-largest-hbo-doc-2010s-1192299/.

525 Variety Staff, "Jackson Concert Sets HBO Record," *Variety*, October 15, 1992, https://varie ty.com/1992/music/news/jackson-concert-sets-hbo-record-101198/.

526 "The Michael Jackson Interview: Oprah Reflects," *Oprah.com*, September 16, 2009, https://www.oprah.com/entertainment/oprah-reflects-on-her-interview-with-michael-j ackson/all.

527 "The President's Tribute to Robert Frost," February 26, 1962, John F. Kennedy Presidential Library and Museum, https://www.jfklibrary.org/asset-viewer/archives/JFKWHA/1962 /JFKWHA-076-002/JFKWHA-076-002.

528 "Remarks at the Ground-Breaking Ceremonies for the Robert Frost Library," October 26, 1963, John F. Kennedy Presidential Library and Museum, https://www.jfklibrary.org/ass et-viewer/archives/JFKWHA/1963/JFKWHA-234-004/JFKWHA-234-004.

529 Prince Jackson interview, *Hotboxin' with Mike Tyson*, August 30, 2023, https://www.youtu be.com/watch?v=6gYAosbGAgs.

530 Kevin Dorsey interview, *MJ Cast*, Episode 115, March 15, 2020, https://www.themjcast.c om/episode-115-kevin-dorsey-special/.

531 Matt Forger interview, *MJ Cast*, Episode 151, December 30, 2022, https://www.themjcast. com/151-matt-forger-special-part-2/.

532 Michael Jackson interview, *Get Music*, 2001, https://www.youtube.com/watch?v=heCJbo s7dfE.

533 Prince Jackson interview, *Nikki Rich Show*, August 23, 2022, https://www.youtube.com/watch?v=nd0HskEubsU.

534 Michael Jackson interview, *Ebony*, 2007, https://www.youtube.com/watch?v=MGPwrBqSrPk.

535 Michael Jackson interview, *Geraldo Rivera*, 2005, https://www.youtube.com/watch?v=7u-Hl_K5nqQ.

536 "Gold Girl Magazine 2002," *True Michael Jackson*, https://www.truemichaeljackson.com/interviews/gold-girl-magazine-2002/.

www.ingramcontent.com/pod-product-compliance
Lightning Source LLC
Chambersburg PA
CBHW030248130626
46549CB00002B/437